371.9043 BEL

Caerleon
Library

BOOK NO: 1754752

KU-504-770

Action Research, Special Needs
and School Development

This book is due for return on or before the last date shown below.

27 MAR 1998	−9. NOV. 2000	2 8 SEP 2007
24. APR 1998	−2 MAR 2001	
	2 0 FEB 2003	
24 APR 1998		
27. MAY 1998	2 4 JAN 2006	
−1 DEC 1998 NOV 1999	2 9 SEP 2006	
−6. MAY 1999	1 2 DEC 2006	
25 MAY 1999		
−6. APR. 2000	1 2 JAN 2007	

Don Gresswell Ltd., London, N.21   Cat. No. 1208   DG 02242/71

CONTRIBUTORS

The contributions were selected from reports of action research conducted by teachers, advisers and support staff in five of the seven networks established since the networking model was first introduced.

The editors were respectively network consultant, user, and adviser; Gordon Bell is Principal and Chief Executive of Bretton Hall College of the University of Leeds, Richard Stakes is Head of Special Needs in a secondary school in Humberside, and Geoff Taylor was General Adviser to Humberside LEA.

List of Editors' other relevant books

Professor Gordon Bell has co-edited with Brian Colbeck *Experiencing Integration: The Sunnyside Action Learning Project*, Falmer 1984 and co-authored *Europe in the School: The School in Europe* with Robert Dransfield (Shell Education Service 1993 His most recent book is *Developing a European Dimension in Primary Schools*, David Fulton 1991.

Action Research, Special Needs and School Development

Edited by Gordon H. Bell
with Richard Stakes and Geoff Taylor

David Fulton Publishers
London

UNIVERSITY OF WALES COLLEGE NEWPORT
LIBRARY AND LEARNING RESOURCES CAERLEON

David Fulton Publishers Ltd
2 Barbon Close, London WC1N 3JX

First published in Great Britain by
David Fulton Publishers 1994

Note: The right of the contributors to be identified as the authors of this work has
been asserted by them in accordance with the Copyright, Designs and Patents Act
1988.

Copyright © David Fulton (Publishers) Limited

British Library Cataloguing in Publication Data

A catalogue record for this book is available from the British Library

ISBN 1-85346-274-8

All rights reserved. No part of this publication may be reproduced, stored in a
retrieval system or transmitted, in any form, or by any means, electronic,
mechanical, photocopying, recording or otherwise without the prior permission of
the publishers.

Designed by Almac Ltd., London
Typeset by Action Typesetting Limited, Gloucester
Printed in Great Britain by the Cromwell Press, Melksham Wilts.

Contents

**PART ONE: ACTION RESEARCH AND SPECIAL
EDUCATIONAL NEEDS**
Richard Stakes

Pupils with Behavioural Problems

**Whole School Policies for Integrating Pupils
with Special Educational Needs**

PART TWO: SCHOOL DEVELOPMENT THROUGH NETWORKING
Gordon H. Bell

Appendices

Foreword

A crucial element in development planning for any school has to be the strategy for supporting and enhancing the learning experience of young people with special educational needs. Around this arise issues about curriculum content and development, staff training and interaction with external expertise that should help shape more general school strategies.

In Humberside action research has provided an innovative and reliable process of staff development which has encouraged schools to think strategically about their response to young people with special educational needs. Whilst primarily achieving development and training for staff it has inevitably dealt very significantly with content and knowledge.

Networks of staff have been set up through several one year cycles that provide a valuable basis for further research and development but also for informal advice and problem solving at a practical level in classrooms and with individual students.

Humberside Local Education Authority has been closely associated with the development of these action research networks in schools. Many colleagues are indebted to Geoff Taylor and Gordon Bell for recognising the potential of this approach and providing consistent support and encouragement. The decision to channel income from the sale of this book to continue to support staff and curriculum development in special educational needs in Humberside is a very welcome sign of the partnership that underwrites these networks.

Dr. M. Garnett
Director of Education, Humberside LEA

Introduction

Geoff Taylor

> It is not enough that teachers' work should be studied, they need to study it themselves. It will require a generation of work (and) the teachers' professional self image and conditions of work will have to change.
>
> Lawrence Stenhouse (1975)

It is sometimes said that new inventions or innovations occur by chance or accident. It was perhaps by chance that a teacher of children with special needs was attending an in-service primary curriculum course where her assignment was to investigate the value of action research in a local authority context for children with special educational needs. The LEA then supported this initial study with a Fellowship for one term and assigned me to be the contact person.

In discussion with the teacher, it became apparent that a network could be established which would comprise a user group of practitioners, a reader group and a support group, and give access to consultants or specialists in research methods or special educational needs. It was quickly realised that someone would be required to co-ordinate such a network.

In response to the evidence presented by the teacher, resources were provided for her to be seconded for two days a week with the brief to establish and co-ordinate an Action Research Network in an area of Humberside. A ready made group of users was found by recruiting colleagues who had undertaken the primary curriculum course. Teachers were approached who expressed an interest in being readers, and consultants were found. At the same time, software and hardware was located with the new co-ordinator so that three databases could be established, the first being a bibliographic database created by using the abstracts produced by the readers. It was established that I would keep a watching brief on the exercise and that Professor Bell would be the project's consultant.

The co-ordinator was seen as the hub of the whole network and she was responsible for establishing a pattern of training meetings for users, supporting them throughout the whole network as well as training readers in the art of abstracting articles. Periodicals which had been purchased for the readers to abstract were held by the co-ordinator and hard copy was provided when identified by the users as being of interest to them in improving their classroom practice.

The end result was regarded as a success. Users were given an opportunity to evaluate the strengths and weaknesses of the network. They all felt supported, valued the access to consultants and even though the database was in its infancy they could appreciate its potential. Those of us who had the opportunity to view the work of the network itself and visit schools where users were working could see the difference that the networking experience had prompted. Teachers felt that they had tackled issues which had been concerning them and had the confidence to prepare teaching programmes to address specific issues and evaluate them. Above all they were prepared to share their experiences with colleagues.

The LEA was impressed with the effectiveness of the network and funding was provided to run Network 2. A teacher who had been a member of the user group for Network 1 was seconded to co-ordinate this network. A recruitment meeting was advertised and from the meeting a user group was formed. Previous users were asked to provide support and additional readers were found. Many of their users were from schools in which members from Network 1 were working. This was seen as an indication of the value of the project.

The network continued the format established by Network 1, but was enhanced by further work on the databases and by the production of the collective reports from its members. All users, supporters, readers, senior officers in the LEA and the consultant received a copy. This particular network was evaluated by the previous co-ordinator as well as the users themselves. It was intended that this should set a pattern of continuity between networks and give an experienced co-ordinator a new role.

The evaluations indicated the need to consider the possibility of offering an award of some kind and this was explored with the LEA. At this time it was suggested that if a teacher was undertaking the locally accredited special needs modular course, the work completed through the Action Research Network could be counted as the equivalent of one module, thus offering the possibility of an exemption.

The advertisement of Network 3 again brought an excellent response from teachers as well as supporters and readers and led to the secondment of another teacher for two days per week to provide co-ordination. Teachers on the modular Special Needs course were given access to the database to support their studies (even though they were not necessarily network members). Once again the established format was followed, databases enhanced and training sessions organised.

The evaluation of this network once more indicated the value of support; access to specialists and the strength of 'belonging', although it also drew attention to the lack of opportunity to achieve an award which was not attached to the modular course. Discussions took place with the project consultant about the possibility of crediting the work within the project in its own right, but at this point it was not seen by the LEA as an arrangement that could be supported financially.

Another teacher was recruited to co-ordinate Network 4 when it was decided to try and associate the research with the implications of meeting special needs within the framework of the National Curriculum. Although many teachers expressed interest in joining the new network, some anxiety was expressed about the amount of extra work in schools with the demands at that time. However, a viable number of users were recruited and again the established format was followed.

The co-ordinator supported the network and was in great demand as a speaker at National Conferences and within other Local Authorities. The database was again used to support Humberside teachers on other courses. One initiative within this Network was the development of a users' handbook which gave up to date information on the network timetable of meetings, people involved and in what capacity, and guidelines on certain techniques which would be required. Another initiative was the setting up of a small supplementary network consisting of teachers working with children in the early years. This nêtwork was destined to run for two years, ably supported by the same co-ordinator.

Discussions took place around this time regarding the development of Action Research networking in other parts of the County. A study was commissioned by the LEA to examine the implications of such a development. The report indicated that in order to provide the amount of co-ordinator time required by a network there would be a need to replicate the provision already available in one of the LEA areas or start again in another. At the same time it was felt that since we had four experienced co-ordinators, those co-ordinators plus the consultant and myself should become an Advisory/Management Group and that each subsequent co-ordinator should become a member of that group on appointment.

It was when the LEA advertised for a co-ordinator for Network 5 that the difficulty of releasing a member of staff for two days a week came to the fore. Headteachers were reluctant to release staff on such a basis. Amongst the reasons given were compensatory funding arrangements where a school might not recoup the full costs for the member of staff, and the need to cover one class with at least two teachers. It became apparent to the Advisory Group that this would be a major stumbling block to any future development, and that what we felt had become a well established and successful format would have to be rethought.

The networks were suspended until proposals could be drawn up and agreed. Eventually it was agreed that it would be possible to reorganise the timetable of the network to allow the co-ordinator to be released full time for one term. Although it meant that preparatory work had to be done in the Autumn Term in the co-ordinator's own time, the bulk of the work would be done with the co-ordinator on secondment during the Spring Term. Reports written by the users would be completed by the beginning of the Autumn Term and collation into a booklet would be undertaken by the subsequent co-ordinator.

These arrangements had a number of advantages and disadvantages. The same arrangements pertained regarding the timetable of meetings and the use of readers, supporters, and consultants, and the co-ordinator was free to make frequent visits to the users in their schools during the time in which their investigations were at their height. Sometimes the co-ordinator taught the class whilst the teacher undertook some investigation with an individual child or the co-ordinator undertook some observation or information gathering for the teacher. A disadvantage was that support was still needed outside the period of the secondment which placed greater stress on the co-ordinator.

The evaluation of Network 5 confirmed the views of the Advisory Group that whilst users appreciated the availability of the co-ordinator during the Spring Term it was felt that support was also needed at other times. Although the Advisory Group discussed these issues at length it was felt that Network 6 should continue with the same format.

The Advisory Group was conscious that one particular area had been extensively canvassed for users and felt that it should be possible to recruit in another. In fact the co-ordinator was able to form networks in two adjacent areas and with the support of members of the Advisory Group was able to sustain support to both. A great deal of interest was shown in the new area and teachers readily accepted the format. The project was strongly supported by consultants within the Learning Support Services and by curriculum support teachers. The additional work load for the co-ordinator led to the appointment of clerical and administrative support. This meant that work on the databases, responding to requests for hard copy, and the typing up of reports could be removed from the co-ordinator leaving her with more time to respond to the needs of the users.

By the time we were recruiting for Network 7 it was increasingly difficult to find resources and attract a co-ordinator to give so much of their own time. More than ever it was apparent that although teachers valued the experience and outcome of the networks, considerably more time and effort was being demanded both in and out of school hours. Reorganisation, National Curriculum, SATS, Curriculum Development, all were taking their toll in extra meetings and providing less time for the normal planning which teachers needed to undertake.

Equally, the changes taking place within other aspects of the Education Service meant that support from the LEA in terms of personnel was not always readily available. However, the LEA still valued the work of the project and a decision was taken to invite an out of county teacher training department to take over the co-ordinating function, and support Networks in two areas.

Network 7 is, at the time of writing, completing its cycle and the groups are maintaining their research, though it has become even more obvious that teachers are under a great deal of pressure and cannot sustain great amounts of additional work.

On reflection, all seven networks have contributed significantly to the development of work with children with special needs in Humberside. Each network brought new developments based on the particular talents of the individual co-ordinators. Many teachers went on to extend their studies on other courses. The team spirit amongst all those who have participated in whatever capacity is still strong. There is hard evidence in the practice in schools that the research undertaken has had substantial effects. The outcomes are well used by teachers and reports are often requested when schools are undertaking some development of their own. Above all, network members are not afraid to identify issues of concern, feel confident to talk to colleagues, construct a line of enquiry, search for possible answers and evaluate the outcomes.

Is this not an increasingly significant part of the role of a professional teacher of children with special educational needs in the decade ahead?

Acknowledgements

The Editors gratefully acknowledge permission to reproduce in Part Two material formerly appearing in the *European Journal of Special Needs Education*. We owe a special debt to all those network members whose work is not represented here for reasons of space, particularly Marilyn Hall and Andrea Todd who contributed greatly to the success of the networks as co-ordinators and evaluators. Mike Wright and Mel Johnson provided valued encouragement and sponsorship throughout for ideas and influences that have their roots in the pioneering work of Lawrence Stenhouse, John Elliott and Don Cooper. Special thanks are also due to Elsie Blackwell and Eileen Watts whose willingness to meet impossible deadlines was superbly matched by their administrative skills, technical competence and good humour.

In editing this collection, we are mindful of the compromises we have had to make in presenting the work of others and in that process may not have fully represented the opinions of individuals or accurately reflected the policy of the employing authorities, agencies or institutions involved. We trust that despite these reservations, the book will stand as a reminder that school development and professional development are inseparably linked and that both are crucially determined by the extent to which teachers can themselves be supported in building a knowledge base of special needs practice. We therefore offer particular thanks to all those who are not identified here who have shared in that commitment and who were and will continue to be essential to this enterprise.

Gordon H Bell, Richard Stakes and Geoff Taylor
Bretton Hall College, University of Leeds
September 1993

PART ONE

Action Research and Special Educational Needs

Richard Stakes

Summary

The projects which were undertaken by teachers in the action research networks have been grouped into five sections:

(1) issues relating to pupils with behavioural problems;
(2) whole school policies for helping better integration;
(3) medical problems which, it was felt, may be related to learning difficulties for particular children;
(4) developing closer liaison between schools in the different phases of schooling, and the school and the home;
(5) learning difficulties in selected areas of the curriculum for individual children

In each of the sections the contributions are discussed in terms of the background of the project, the action steps taken, the results and evaluation of this action, and a summary of conclusions. This structure attempts to reflect the processes of action research as shown in Figure 1 on the next page.

No attempt has been made to make comparisons. Even though some of these projects are on superficially similar topics, this was felt to be inappropriate particularly as the circumstances which prevailed in each school were unique. This is not to say, however, that lessons cannot be drawn from each case, or that adaptations and developments do not arise for testing in other situations.

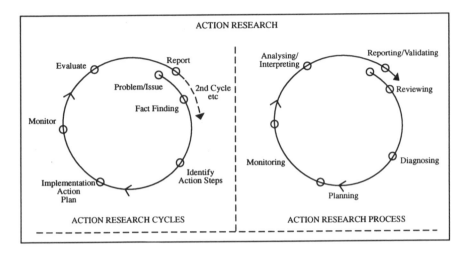

Pupils with Behavioural Problems

It is a tradition of English education that classroom teachers take responsibility for the control and academic development of the children in their class. Further it is acknowledged that they undertake to resolve any difficulties in the most appropriate way. In the light of this, and the evidence provided by those such as Reynolds (1976) Rutter et al (1979) and Mortimore et al (1988) indicating that the teacher and the school can significantly influence the behaviour of pupils, it is hardly surprising that a number of contributors to the action research networks concentrated on attempts to alleviate such problems exhibited by certain of their pupils.

The projects reported in this section were undertaken by teachers working in primary schools. Major (1988) looked at the issue of disaffected and disruptive children. In the following network (Major, 1989), she tackled the relationship between motivation and self-esteem in a group of children at her school. Cawkwell (1990) undertook some work on behaviour modification and peer group tutoring of a disruptive pupil in her class. Linsley (1988) traced links with reading progress whilst for Morling (1990), the problem selected was related to taking over a new class in mid-year with a number of difficult pupils in it. Webb (1991), although undertaking work with a group of Year 6 pupils, provided a model which could be adapted for use with other age groups.

1. Disaffected and Disruptive Behaviour

J. Major (1988)

Background

One of the consequences of the teachers' role in taking responsibility for a group of children in their care is that disruptive children can be a cause of stress to their teachers as well as wasting the time of their classmates.

All three of the pupils chosen for this project were boys. Two of the boys were statemented, and one was awaiting a placement in a residential unit. The boys were aged eleven, ten and seven. Each had brothers and sisters and although none came from excessively large family groupings, the children had a long history of poor behaviour dating back to the nursery school. Major reported that their behaviour was disruptive to other children and that they were unable to accept the discipline imposed by their teachers. Two of them were also described as being of 'low academic ability'.

Action Research

From the records of the pupils concerned, an analysis of the children's behavioural pattern was undertaken with the assistance of their previous teachers. To facilitate this a five point chart after Fisher (mimeo) was used which outlined positive approaches to behavioural problems. This approach indicated that such points as the daily routine of the child, the relationship with adults and their peer group, their personal behaviour and their immediate environment were factors which should be considered in implementing such a programme.

As a further source of information, a sociogram of the three classes where each of these children were taught was conducted. This was done to ascertain if any of the target group could be supported by a peer. The results showed this was not possible as none of them were chosen by any members of their peer groups. However each of them was able to choose one child with whom they felt they could work.

These choices proved interesting. One of them selected a timid individual who was afraid of him, the second picked an intelligent, quiet, well-behaved boy, while the third chose a motherly girl who frequently helped him with his work and gave him food.

Major described the next part of the project as 'most illuminating and useful'. This was a twenty minute observation of each child. This was done in co-operation with each of the class teachers. The boys were observed during a period of 'desk work' so that it would be easier to 'monitor the periods when the children were on task as they had no call to move around the room or discuss work in groups'.

Outcomes

In the case of the eldest boy, A, the results showed that he spent so little time 'on task' that there was small wonder his work was careless and disjointed. It pinpointed his desire for adult attention in any form that he could attract it. He constantly followed the teacher's movements and listened to her remarks to other children, interrupting at intervals. B was shown to be unaware of his 'funny noises' at times as he did not seem to be trying to engage the teacher's attention but often made the sound when he was on task and fully involved. Both these children presented facial grimacing to a much greater extent than their peers. The grimaces were not directed at anyone and were not apparently used to attract attention. C was given instant attention to his every demand either by his peers or his teacher. This may have been expedient in preventing temper tantrums which occurred if he encountered difficulties or had to wait for attention. However, this may have caused further problems as he came to expect instant gratification. His peer group were very accommodating in their treatment of him and at that time showed no sign of resentment at his pushing to the front or receiving extra attention.

In much of the literature, reward systems are advocated. For instance The Association of Education Psychologists (1983) stated 'rewards of all kinds should be encouraged and given out as often as possible thereby placing the whole emphasis of the school on achievement, effort and positive aspects of life in general'. Positive reinforcers are the most effective way of teaching new behaviour patterns. 'Rewards should be immediate, consistent and abundant positive reinforcers. These can include teacher attention, praise, and preferred activities (giving children time for activities they prefer to do provided they complete their work assignments). Contrived reinforcers, stars, tokens, sweets, etc, are useful when a child cannot cope with any long term postponement of feedback. Token rewards can also be used as bridges to more long term reinforcements'. These contrived reinforcers can take the form of any objects or visible marks which are easy to see and handle but are neither easy to copy nor readily available elsewhere. Further, they have advantages in that they allow teachers to reward immediately for small incremental changes in behaviour and they may be exchanged to allow the child to choose a special privileged activity or use of apparatus.

At this stage it was necessary to ascertain which type of reward each child should receive. Some disruptive pupils are clearly not concerned with pleasing the teacher and are less likely to respond positively to praise which may be counter productive if the pupil resents the teacher's comments as this may destroy their image with their peers. Praise is more likely to be effective educationally if it focuses on the work rather than the child as a person, if it describes the behaviour which is being reinforced and is perceived to be sincere and justified.

It was felt that it would be expedient to discover reward preferences which would be most meaningful to the individual, following Branwhite (1990) who suggests that any serious attempt to boost performance clearly requires careful management of variables which will determine how the child is to be instructed and motivated. These he argued, must include some kind of positive pay off strategy i.e. tangible or social rewards, contingent upon learning.

The three children completed a questionnaire (with help) to further the study. This resulted in child C choosing to be rewarded by his class teacher and to choose token rewards, while the older boys chose male members of staff and 'preferred activity' time. Child B chose Her Majesty the Queen as his first choice and then the Headmaster!

Conclusions

When initiating this scheme again in the future, Major indicated she will use the following strategies:

> Each child will be given a small book with a section for each period of the day (reducing to morning and afternoon sessions if successful). The class teacher will discuss the piece of behaviour to be monitored with the child. (It is most unreasonable to expect to remediate all the behaviours at one fell swoop). The class teacher will then indicate in the book when the child has complied with the request but leave the space blank if the problem behaviour has occurred.

The reward book will be taken daily by the older boys to their chosen person. Rewards of preferred activities of ten to fifteen minutes duration will be given and further time may be earned by the children.

2. A Token Reward System

S. Cawkwell (1990)

Background

In the classroom, the child D was described as inconsistent and unpredictable. He lacked concentration and was very restless. He was disruptive and annoyed other children. He could also be aggressive. He needed close supervision to attempt tasks and he found difficulties with daily routines. He liked to be with adults on a one-to-one basis and could be helpful at these times. Relationships with peers were very volatile e.g. he had special friends at one time, but that could change a few minutes later. After he had done wrong he knew it. Sometimes he owned up to the fact but more often than not he tried to talk his way out of it, or blamed somebody else.

Cawkwell worked on similar problems to those described by Major (above). The subject was an eight year old boy with a reading age assessed at six yrs seven mths (Salford Scale) and a score of 16−E on the Quest Number Test. The Aston Index indicated that he had memory problems with both auditory and visual factors. He was shown to have concentration problems which may have compounded his learning difficulties. She indicated that there had been no parental contact and that the boy's disruptive behaviour pattern had been first observed in the infant school.

Action Research

In trying to help D with his difficulties, the following actions were initiated: a ten minute observation session, the completion of a Self-Image chart and the Piers Harris Self Concept Sheet and a checklist was produced for recording classroom observations.

Outcomes

The results of these activities indicated that during the ten minute observation the child did not work. He wandered around annoying other children, went back to his table, dropped his pencil, went up to the teacher, kicked the bin whilst waiting, went away and employed various diversionary tactics until the teacher had to intervene between D and another child.

The self image chart indicated that D was a happy person most of the time, but he didn't like it when people made fun of him because he couldn't do the work. He thought that he was clever because he came to school. D didn't think he was shy or nervous and thought that when he grew up he would be very important.

D knew he wasn't well behaved and said he caused trouble at home because he didn't think he was important there. Further, he didn't want to change his appearance as he liked the way he looked. He said he had lots of friends who were boys because he liked to fight with them and play football. He claimed that the other boys always started the fights because they picked on him.

Using the Piers Harris version of the Self-Image questionnaire, he was questioned orally. By the age of eight, self attitudes have a reasonable amount of stability and responses should adequately reflect the child's general self concepts.

D said he liked watching television a lot and watched lots of videos. When he saw the picture of the girl with the football in the questionnaire he said he really liked playing football 'the best thing in the world'. He played football in the playground at every opportunity and became very upset if he was not chosen for a team. He appeared to enjoy coming to school. He was always punctual and very rarely had time off because of illness. D said he liked writing but it took a long time. He would like to be able to read car magazines like his Dad did at night. He would also like to build cars with his Dad who worked for a local car company.

In written work, D copied correctly and his letters were reasonably formed although very small. He preferred verbal to written instructions and he appeared attentive at times but more often than not squirmed about on his seat or played with things on his desk. He was very willing to participate in all class activities, especially art/craft work, C.D.T, computer work or helping the teacher. In an attempt to alleviate the situation, D's misdemeanours were written down in order with the worst at the top to decide which behaviour needed modifying first. There were two main concerns; wandering around the classroom annoying other children and playing up whilst the teacher was helping other children.

It was important that consistent strategies of behavioural management were set up. As D responded to reward systems, rewards were given whenever he stayed in his place. The teacher researcher tried to ignore him when he was out of his place (unless actually disrupting other children). Special work was given with modified demands, divided into small steps, to try to increase teacher time approving work and encouraging each small piece of work – hopefully working to pave the way for regular positive contact. D responded well to the fact that the teacher went up to see him when he was working; so standing near became added encouragement. Praise was given quickly and consistently making sure that it was for specific approved behaviour.

A reward system was devised consisting of a star for every lesson. If he achieved four stars in one day D would have his star book plus a sticker to take home. This reward system had to be modified as a lesson proved to be too long a duration. For if D did not behave well in the morning he had no chance of a sticker later, so he didn't try.

However, despite this strategy being introduced, it was clear that D still needed a lot of attention, so Peer Group Tutoring was introduced.

There were various learning theories that were taken into account in developing the programme. These included the Role Model Theory — (which implies that tutees are more likely to learn from their peers than from teachers who are viewed as coming from another culture), the Gestalt theory (which implies that learning will occur when the learner 'locates' an item in an intellectual structure and where tutors have to reflect on what they have learned to be able to represent it to their tutees and thereby master it better) and the Behaviourist Theory (which suggests that learning will be efficient if every correct response to a question by a pupil is rewarded in order to act as a stimulus to make another step in learning). As tutoring offered rapid reinforcement of learning it was hoped that tutees would benefit from being tutored by receiving individual instruction thus receiving more teaching, responding to their peers and experiencing companionship from their tutors.

The tutors may learn by reviewing, filling in gaps in their own learning, and consolidating knowledge or learning through a process of reformulation. Moreover, peer tutoring releases the teacher from more routine tasks and if a peer helper is able to provide almost instant support then the special needs pupil's behaviour problems will decrease. Learning will therefore increase if every response a learner makes received instant feedback. Secondly, with two peer helpers, it reduces the risk of possible annoyance at being disturbed.

To attempt to find a friendship tutor for D, all the children in the class were given a piece of paper and asked to write down three favourite friends, in order of preference. Points were awarded as follows:

1st name — 3 points
2nd name — 2 points
3rd name — 1 point

The order was then recorded on a friendship chart. The results indicated that D was chosen by two children as 2nd and 3rd choice friend, but interestingly not by either of the two children he chose. The children who chose D had modest academic ability.

The two children D chose were noisy and disruptive on occasion with playground behaviour being a particular problem. They were also the two most popular boys amongst those in the class — the ones that organised football games at playtime.

Ideally D should have peer tutors who were his close friends, but unfortunately this would not work as they were too easily distracted themselves. Matching D's needs was therefore planned with two children of average ability being chosen to help with most activities.

After initiating this programme, D tried at first to demand their almost constant attention to talk about anything and everything. During the first two days he barely put pen to paper. Instructions were given to the peer helpers, in his hearing, that they could only help D if his questions related to the work that he was doing. D became really restless during the next few days and started to take the other children's belongings and throw them on the floor. He generally went out of his way to annoy the other two children, particularly if they were working. He would get out of his place to wander to his 'friends', and to look out of the windows at the back of the classroom at frequent intervals. The two peer helpers showed remarkable patience with D over these incidents and said 'It's just D, he's always like it!'

During the next week, D started to work for very short periods of approximately five minutes on his new maths book and also on his new English work. This was immediately praised and he found it easier having someone next to him he could ask about his work. His stars on the reward system increased rapidly and he started to stay round his table for up to half an hour at a time before wandering off.

D then began to see the children could be of great use to him, and he began to demand that they actually do the work for him! When he realised that wouldn't work after nearly a day of sulking and temper tantrums he decided to try again himself.

After the system had been in operation for twenty days, D had become more settled and was working for up to fifteen minutes at a time with a break for the usual fiddling in his tray, dropping things on the floor, wandering about etc. During lesson times, D's wanderings had lessened considerably to around his own table and occasionally to the sink, supposedly to wash his hands. (This process could take ten minutes as he loved to play with water).

As many of the reasons for movement as possible had been eliminated. The teacher now went across to him when he put his hand up although obviously there were times when this could not happen immediately, and D reverted to tilting back on his chair and dropping things whilst he was waiting, but on the whole he stayed in his place.

D had a peer tutor for reading and had already read three books in two and a half weeks as opposed to one a month. He had also started doing the corresponding work and was quite proud of the stars he was achieving. He could read the next few pages of the book only if he had done the written work linked with it, and he managed to read two or three pages a day.

Maths work varied tremendously but D managed on 'good' days to achieve 20–25 sums, but on bad days maybe only five. This rate increased with practical maths but could only be sustained for fifteen to twenty minutes at a time, as then he started to interfere with the apparatus, so the activity was usually kept short. With the computer work, the peer tutors were invaluable as the discussions between the three children were frequently of more benefit than the actual result of the programme.

Over the next few weeks stable relationships began to be formed. When one of the helpers was ill, D became more restless and demanding of the other peer helper until she returned. It was decided after this incident not to let D become too dependent on one specific helper and to use different peer helpers for different tasks. At the time, D only had two peer helpers for class work (plus one for reading). This was extended to interactive pairs, one for Art, one for Design and Technology and one for P.E. and Games.

The reward system was also improved upon by using a piece of card folded in half with a space station and aliens on each side. On the one side good points were coloured in and on the other side the bad behaviour points – the aim being to fill up the positive side first!

Conclusions

D was beginning to stay in his place for longer periods of time, remaining on task for increasing lengths of time and improving his reading dramatically. Relationships with other children were improving, with far less aggression in the classroom, although there were still many problems in the playground. Further, he had begun to realise that bad behaviour was unacceptable and he managed to control himself better. The results of the new reward system linked to the existing one, helped in this, as D was desperate to fill up the good side first. (Bad points were only given under extreme provocation unless he was annoying other children. D realised this and tried to avoid these situations in the classroom).

D responded well to this reward system whilst the different pairs of children enjoyed working together perhaps because different thinking styles and views could be shared in co-operation rather than in competition.

The effectiveness of support appeared to depend on the length of time spent by peer helpers supporting 'special needs' pupils, the match between 'special needs' and helpers, and whether the enthusiasm could be maintained both by the children and the teacher. Cawkwell concluded that on the whole she found that practical tasks appeared to be more suited to a peer tutoring approach.

3. Breaking the Failure Spiral

R. Linsley (1988)

Background

In this project the teacher researcher attempted to tackle poor classroom behaviour in conjunction with developing reading skills.

The pupil (C) was described in the following terms:

> This was a boy who had already acquired a name for being involved in most playground incidents, having little motivation for work of any type, being below average in reading, although not sufficiently to be regarded as in need of remedial support, and unable to sustain concentration for very long. Although I was relating my investigation to one child, I felt that this was a worthy area for study as it is a problem which I have met on many occasions before, namely those children who are above the level at which they are felt to be in need of special attention, but who produce little work and of poor quality, often exhibit aggressive behaviour towards other children, and yet something suggests that there is more about them. Often such children display better than average general knowledge, or knowledge in a particular field which interests them. Often they seem to relate well to adults on a one to one basis.

She decided to look carefully at the factors contributing to his behaviour and his reactions to various situations. She wished to try various strategies and evaluate them to see if they favourably affected his behaviour.

Action Research

Firstly she wrote down what the staff knew of his background and family. Being a fairly small school it was possible to do this in an informal discussion. At this stage she consulted an LEA adviser for Special Educational Needs. With his help she targeted reading as a first area of investigation; she hoped that if his self image in this area could be improved it might have repercussions across a broader spectrum. At the suggestion of the adviser, she checked for gaps in C's sight vocabulary using the McNally 100 Keywords list and found 28 unknown words. She also checked his phonic skills, beginning with single letter sounds and names, and then initial consonant blends. The test showed that he was secure on all but two letter sounds, but that he had significant gaps in initial consonant blends. She decided to tackle these and then continue testing further at a later date.

For her action plan, she made a set of base and matching cards using the 100 keywords, and employed these with C and four other children of similar ability to play pelmanism type games. Collectively, they were able to read almost all of the words and run the game themselves.

She began making a particular point when listening to C read to focus his attention on the parts of words which he was failing on and found that his ability to decode increased. Further, she devised an individual phonic programme for C using a combination of East Riding Remedial Service cards, and cards from the Hull Remedial Service scheme, targeting those initial blends which her tests had shown him to be deficient in.

A Language Master was then introduced into the classroom to assist C and others in the acquisition of sight words and phonic blends. She began by making individual cards cut to length of the 28 keywords which C did not know and likewise the initial consonant blends. In order that the Language Master was not seen by other children as something for 'failures', it was introduced to the whole class, and each child in turn was allowed to spend time listening to the words and sounds. She had recorded the tapes herself as it is important that sounds are presented to the children in a familiar voice. A turn on the Language Master was regarded as a treat and a set of 'fair rules' was devised to ensure equal turns. This was good as it was seen as prestigious rather than degrading to be sent to the Language Master for ten minutes.

Once the initial interest had been satisfied it was explained that anyone could use the Language Master to revise a word or sound. However its use was concentrated on C and other children with similar difficulties. For his first session she allowed him to experiment, and at the end of the session, to bring to her two things which he had learnt. Thereafter, a session began by identifying as many as possible of the previous day's words, and depending on the success rate, new words were added at the rate of two or three a day.

At the suggestion of the LEA adviser C undertook the Digit Repetition Test (test and instructions in Westwood, 1975). Results showed that he could cope with four consecutive digits, five evoked an uncertain response, and six were completely beyond him. The class played games which involved sequencing. An interesting result was that his success rate was considerably higher when he had clues in the form of words. C was chosen to run errands, giving him instructions to carry out which he had to remember and sequence. He proved quite successful at this. At weekly intervals sight vocabulary was re-checked, using just those words which he had previously mis-cued.

Outcomes

Linsley stated she had begun with the idea of improving C's self-image by improving his view of himself as a reader. Her first step, therefore in analyzing her data, was to look for occurrences of comments related to success. Several factors seemed to emerge. These included indications that his success rate appeared to increase when his attention was carefully focused on the parts of a word with which he was having trouble.

He mis-cued words when read from card, but could easily read them from the Language Master. This is a factor which has also been noticed when children are using word processors and reading from a vertical screen. They appear to find words easier to decode in this form, and this could be of importance when looking for strategies to help children like C.

He worked better in a small group overseen by an adult where he was not aware of other groups near him. For children like C, learning experiences which gradually expose them to such situations would be valuable. He worked well on small, well-defined tasks, often individually tailored to his requirements. This obviously has importance in terms of the sort of tasks with which he was subsequently presented.

The incidence of comments related to his success increased as the action research cycle progressed. This suggested perhaps that his self-image was improving and that the failure spiral had been broken for a little while and replaced with a success spiral. The important, but difficult thing, was to make this the case long term.

At weekly intervals when the mis-cued keywords were checked, improvements were noted. After one week, the initial twenty-eight had reduced to fourteen, none of which were words previously known. Linsley stated she did not feel that she had done sufficient extra work on these words with C to account solely for this increased success, and looked for other factors which might be responsible. He had recently acquired his glasses, but she felt she had not got sufficient evidence to support this possible explanation.

Subsequent checks on his sight vocabulary revealed that after four weeks, there were just eight words with which he was still having difficulty.

Another factor which she had felt to be relevant in her initial assessment of the problem was C's inconsistent level of reading, something which had also been referred to by his previous teacher. On looking at the results from the regular checks made on the keywords she had to concede that his responses were quite consistent, only four words being read correctly on one occasion, and incorrectly at a later date. A third factor was her revised attitude to C, or maybe his revised perception of her attitude to him. This was borne out by his mother's comment at a parents' night. The mother claimed that for the first time since C began school, he was coming happily, talking with enthusiasm about what he was doing, and expressing liking for school.

One interesting connection did emerge from the observational record. On an initial read-through it was noted that a reference to disruptive behaviour was followed by an illness. Therefore she decided to look at the correlation between incidents of disruptive or aggressive behaviour and illness. On two occasions this proved to be the case, and on one other, aggressive behaviour occurred just before he began to wear glasses. Hardly conclusive, but a definite indicator to look for in the future. In relation to his behaviour, it also emerged that aggressive incident became less frequent as the programme progressed. It would be necessary to see if this was a continuing trend, but it appeared that the initial objective was on the way to being achieved.

Conclusions

The attention to detail which was employed in the formulation of the action plan accounted in large measure for its success. The very fact of being involved in the network caused a re-appraisal of the way of assessing the children's needs, and also how she set about fulfilling those needs.

Her initial feeling that there was room for improvement had been justified. After only four weeks, C was showing that he was capable of more than he had been producing and this was the foundation for further progress.

Carefully targeting small areas for study at one time was found to be an effective way of bringing about improvement. In terms of the steps taken, the work done seemed insignificant but there had been a real improvement in C's attitude and work.

Improving his self-image appeared to increase expectations. For as C began to experience success and to realise that he was being praised because of his efforts, so his own desire to produce well presented work increased.

Unanswered questions remained. There was the issue of the relation between health and the standard of work. This was something which could usefully be monitored in the future. On some occasions, C's writing contained many reversals, mixed up words and misformed letters; on other days he produced well presented work. She asks: are the causative factors physical, emotional or the result of mood or attitude? Are they things which can be affected by the school's approach, or are they related to his home circumstances? Questions which could form the basis of further action research.

4. Motivation and Self Esteem in Deprived Children

J.Major (1989)

Background

Similarly to Linsley (report 3), this teacher researcher wished to link the issue of self esteem with the improvement of reading skills amongst the least able children. She particularly wished to involve parents in this strategy and wanted to initiate a paired reading scheme based on the work of Topping and McKnight (1984) guide-lines provided by the National Association of Remedial Education (1988).

Initially Major administered, with the help of colleagues, a social deprivation questionnaire to all the pupils in her school. The result of this survey indicated that 30 per cent of the pupils were eligible for free school meals, 20 per cent came from large families (four children or more), 10 per cent of the children had one parent or came from split families, 6 per cent required the help of a social worker, and 7 per cent received help from child guidance for both educational and behavioural problems. Further, some 28 per cent had experienced school transfer other than the move from the feeder infant school.

Action Research

This project was directed towards a group of twenty first-year junior children who later took part in a paired reading scheme. It involved looking at their motivation, access to reading material, parental involvement with reading and self esteem. The results of this study were followed up six months to one year after the paired reading project.

Ten children were chosen from the poorest readers as tested on Young's Group Reading Test prior to entry to the school by the LEA Learning Support Service. A control group of ten good readers was selected from the same test results. Both groups were re-tested using the same tests. The results showed gains of one to three months in seven months for the poor readers and three to thirteen months for the control group. It was interesting to note that two children from the control group had made no progress during this period and both experienced difficult home circumstances. This bears out the point made by Vernon (1971) that fear of danger, illness or homelessness can take away much interest in school activities or make the effort to work hard.

The second stage involved the use of questionnaires to ascertain the children's attitude to school subjects, particularly reading. Questions were also posed to find the extent of parental involvement with reading, adult reading models and access to reading material. The questions were read to both groups of children to ensure they were understood. While the children were being questioned they were given simple drawing tasks to put them at ease.

The questionnaires were adapted from two used by the LEA special needs support service. Major anticipated a tendency for children to give the answers expected of them and therefore used the pictorial check list at the second interview. The results of both questionnaires were remarkably similar.

Outcomes

The results of the questionnaire indicated that one child from each group disliked school. Both children were experiencing difficult social circumstances. Five poor readers disliked reading and writing. All the control group enjoyed both activities . Every child in the survey enjoyed art and craft. This indicates that an approach through art may stimulate the readers. Three poor readers felt that reading was unimportant but only one thought he would not need to read as an adult.

Two children thought they would not need to read at work. Every child in the control group recognised the importance of reading now and in adulthood. Surprisingly, three of the control group thought they wouldn't need to read at work. This may indicate limited expectations already forming at seven and a half to eight years of age.

Two poor readers were without books and three didn't read at home. These findings bear out the generally held view that cultural deprivation particularly affects language abilities and hence reading progress. All the control group had books at home and read. Neither group showed much interest in comics or magazines. They may not have had access to these because of limited incomes at home.

Very few visited the public library either alone or with parents. This fact echoed studies which showed very marked differences between good and poor readers in the number of adult books and newspapers in the home and in the frequency of membership of public libraries. Four mothers and no fathers read books in the poor readers' group. In the control group all mothers and three fathers read books. The responses concerning parental involvement with reading were the most disturbing especially considering the age of the children concerned. Bearing in mind the point made by Durkin (1966) that an influential factor in reading progress in the U.S.A. is parents reading to their children, this survey indicated that while only four mothers and no fathers read to the poor group, three mothers and three fathers read to the control group. Newsom and Newsom (1963) found that fathers and mothers of good readers often told their children bedtime stories. The response to this questionnaire showed a picture of deprivation, a lack of stimulation in the home, lack of parental co-operation with school and low aspirations for their children.

The Self Esteem questionnaire proved to be the most interesting and informative part of the research. The local Child Guidance Service provided access to two self-image inventories; the Piers Harris Children's Self Concept Scale, and James Battle's Culture Free Self Esteem Inventory. Advice on their use and interpretation was also given.

The decision to use the Harris version was made because of the complexity of the Battle questions which contained negatives which were confusing to the children. The answers to both questionnaires allowed no flexibility of response. Piers Harris defends the omission of a 'maybe' or 'uncertain' response as he found that children would overuse it and so reduce the meaningfulness of the results. However he admits that it may force children to endorse items which are not really descriptive of them.

For the purpose of this research the questions fitting the following categories were extracted: Popularity, School Status, Behaviour, Anxiety, and Home Status.

The children were questioned orally and individually so that it was possible to reframe questions and monitor responses. The questionnaire was not particularly time consuming and the children appeared to enjoy the one-to-one relationship and the opportunity to talk about themselves. Requests had been made to come and talk again.

The responses to questions were difficult to interpret as they depended on the child's personal understanding of the question and the tendency of young children not to relate their answers to past experience but to give a purely momentary response. For example 'Are you happy?' can depend on the day's events. Moreover, convention was observed by some children in the control group when asked about cleverness and personal appearance. Several children were quite embarrassed and reluctant to answer.

However, the children were also very reluctant to admit to bad behaviour. Harris states that 'By the age of eight, self attitudes have a reasonable amount of stability and responses should adequately reflect the child's general self concepts.'

The results of this survey indicated that in relation to the popularity factor two of the poorer readers had low scores in the Harris test while three had very low scores and four average scores. The control group showed that seven had high scores and three average scores indicating that among the group the poor readers had a greater tendency towards difficulties in social relationships than those in the control group.

The school status category indicated that the poor readers had average scores and seven high scores, whilst the control group had four with average scores, three with good scores and three with high scores. This result indicates that the pupils selected for this survey did not, at this stage, have major problems with their status in school, and did not feel they were failing or unimportant there.

The scores from the behaviour category indicated four poor readers with average scores while six had very good scores. In the control group only one had an average score while nine had very good scores. Again the results obtained by the target group can be seen to have been positive although Harris has pointed out 'it is our impression that with young children in particular the desire to "look good" is fairly strong but rather than being a deliberate attempt to mislead, their responses reflect a confusion between how they really feel and how they have been told they should feel'.

The anxiety scores indicated that three pupils in the target group had high anxiety scores, four had average scores and three low anxiety scores. The control group however showed four with average scores and six with low anxiety scores. These results indicated an important difference between the two groups – 70 per cent of the target group with average and above scores and with only 40 per cent of the control group being in that category.

The anxiety expressed by the pupils concerned their parents or their siblings. No child in either group expressed anxiety about school. Lytton (1968) has indicated that poor readers can be distinguished by a lower drive level in a reading task and by higher degrees of anxiety and by a more adverse parental relationship. Meanwhile, Fraser (1959) obtained a correlation of 66 per cent between parental encouragement and school achievement. This was a higher correlation than with anything else he tested in his survey.

Conclusions

In terms of an analysis of the children's home status, two of the poor readers suggested that they felt they were unimportant in their family and four children felt that their parents were disappointed with them. The control group indicated that four children felt they were unimportant in their family whilst none felt their parents were disappointed with them. Again this part of the survey indicated that the target group generally had feelings of lower status and worth in their family than the other group of children.

In the light of this evidence a paired reading project was initiated to start the next term and to involve all the target group.

5. Disruptive Behaviour in the Infant Classroom

L.Morling (1991)

Background

This teacher researcher working with the infant age group range was particularly concerned with behavioural problems in a class which she took over in the middle of a school year.

These pupils were regarded within the school as a 'difficult' class. Before Christmas, four children had been withdrawn to work with the head teacher each morning and five pupils had been referred to a disaffected centre. These particular children were very disruptive and caused a lot of problems.

Prior to starting with the class, strategies to help improve behaviour were drawn up with the special needs co-ordinator and this was verified by the Child Psychologist. The strategies involved the class drawing up rules of acceptable behaviour which would then enable anyone to earn increased access to preferred activities such as PE, Gymnastics, baking etc. Classroom management aimed to lessen problems with the disruptive children being seated on separate tables without eye contact. There was also to be a positive approach, trying to ignore attention seeking behaviour and giving plenty of praise for good social behaviour, settling down to work etc. If these strategies were insufficient, parental involvement would be used and 'smile charts' introduced.

She found the times for talking and listening and for stories in large groups very difficult. Some of the behaviours exhibited were shouting out, throwing things, poking each other, talking loudly to each other and making irritating noises. Several children found it difficult to listen to her or anyone else.

She felt these behaviours put up a barrier to learning and made it very difficult to deliver many areas of the National Curriculum.

Various parts of the established literature yielded ideas on developing speaking and listening skills. For example, the 'English Studies Centre', comment that 'few adults can listen to each other with patience so it is unrealistic to expect children to do so'. This implied that she should make it as easy as possible to listen to her and each other.

Teachers rarely allow for continuous dialogue yet new thinking in children nearly always accompanies talking with someone. What often happens is to fire questions at children accepting the right answer and then fire another question. An alternative approach suggests a form of debate in which all or most of the children engage, speaking one at a time and directly to the previous speaker not via the teacher. The teacher researcher felt she was not letting this happen and thought that varying their talk times might enable this to happen. The reasons for talk were having someone to talk to, having something to say, having something to learn, having an audience, having something interesting to discuss, having something worthwhile to achieve, having fun with language, and having the need to talk. It was felt that all these ideas had a place for helping the children vary their talk patterns.

Other people had ideas to contribute. The Action Research Network members provided the idea of the speaker holding a teddy or equivalent in order to control the situation. The suggestion was also made of putting spots on a large wall-mounted dragon as a reward for good behaviour. In addition, a great deal of support came from an out-worker from the local pupil withdrawal centre. From the special needs co-ordinator came the idea of drawing up rules for appropriate behaviour for sitting on the carpet where group talk time took place. The children were to give the input for this. Emphasis was to be given to ignoring poor behaviour and praising good behaviour. The idea of smile charts for general behaviour modification, which had special areas for talk times and story times, were to be introduced. Parents were to become involved in this revised approach.

Action Research

These ideas did not all come at once but over a period of time. However the strategy was to try to introduce each new idea in turn. Time intervals were recorded in order to monitor how long the pupils were able to sit and talk without a serious interruption, whenever a new strategy was introduced. The first part of the morning session and storytime in the afternoon were the times chosen to record responses.

The first step was to draw up rules for appropriate behaviour when sitting on the carpet.The children said what they thought should happen, the worst offenders making the most contributions. The rules were: hands up to talk, talk one at a time, only sensible behaviour was allowed, i.e. they were not to fight, throw anything around etc. These rules were written out and put on a cupboard next to the carpet.

All attention seeking behaviour was ignored, (silly noises etc); behaviour was praised which kept to the rules. A way of praising quiet entry into the room was to pick four sitting quietly on the carpet to sit on four soft chairs, which otherwise they would fight over. Those who had kept the rules had first choice of activities i.e. they could pick which table they went to first, when talk time was finished, which they regarded as a privilege. If the whole class had sat well this was rewarded a few minutes extra play or extra PE.

The children were encouraged to question each other. More small group work was introduced to give them more chance to talk and listen. Having an audience, e.g. showing things made in Technology or reading out a story was tried and this was a success for one particular child. One day a 'feely box' was used and they had to describe to each other what they had found. This practised language, questioning, listening and sitting according to the rules. Only those doing this got a turn.

It was considered important to ensure there were interesting things to talk about, e.g. various animals were brought for them to talk about and as a way of having fun with language, Roald Dahl stories (originally *The Twits* and *George's Marvellous Medicine*) were introduced. Close physical contact was also tried. The worst behaved child liked to sit close and hold hands, while another also liked to be close.

When one child got very difficult his behaviour was monitored very closely and a spot was put on a dragon for every five minutes good behaviour; getting enough spots gave him a smile on his smile chart.

An overall behaviour modification programme had to be introduced, initially for three boys and then for two more a little later on. As part of the programme the children had charts divided up into parts of the day, and smiley faces or equivalents, cars, pigeons and spiders were given for good behaviour. Parents, who were all keen to co-operate, rewarded by giving pocket money when it was deserved. One area of the chart was specifically used for rewarding good behaviour in talking and listening times and storytime.

Outcomes

The rules made a minimal difference − they kept reminding each other of them although not always obeying them. Ignoring attention seekers helped although this was very difficult. One child was a case in point as he made silly noises and then looked to see what would be done. Eventually over time he did stop. The very negative actions of putting children outside and making them miss playtime stopped them interrupting, as they valued their playtime. This was something done in the early days on rare occasions because an individual could make it impossible for others to gain essential information.

Being picked for a chair was an extremely good way of making a quiet start to a session. Rewarding good behaviour by choosing an activity took a very long time to get through to the problem children, although they complained bitterly if they were last to be picked. It did however reward those who always behaved.

Talking and questioning each other gave peaceful sessions as they were prepared to wait quietly to have a turn to ask. Repositioning them into a circle so that they could see each other was relevant for this type of session. Talking to an audience encouraged the audience to listen as they were keen to have their turn as speakers and knew they would only get it if they kept to the rules. They very much enjoyed showing their work or reading stories and developed a pleasing tolerance of the varying standards of work within the class. On one occasion silence reigned, apart from the required speakers for half an hour. A reward was given that day!

Using funny stories kept all the children enthralled, *The Twits*, *George's Marvellous Medicine*, *Charlie and the Chocolate Factory* being their favourites. These gave some very enjoyable story times, replacing the times of stress in the early days.

Physical contact helped with one child who was a very serious problem; it gave everyone a quiet time if he held the teacher's hand; not something to encourage normally, but if he didn't have attention that way he'd find other less desirable ways.

Holding up a teddy bear was a great help and a novelty and lessened calling out whilst it was their turn to hold him. Someone was sure to fetch him off the shelf if the teacher forgot.

Putting spots on a dragon helped a little in one child's overall programme, as he knew that if he didn't get enough spots he didn't get his smile for that session and consequently his reward when he got home.

Morling felt that the biggest contributor to solving the behavioural problem she encountered was the 'smile' chart (with the exception of one child whose family's catastrophes got worse and worse.) All the parents involved said their children were easier to deal with at home and they began to improve substantially in all areas at school. Meanwhile talking and listening times and storytimes certainly became better.

Conclusions

All in all, things got better in the classroom and pupils became happier and more relaxed. However there were several setbacks along the way. The most difficult child arrived back after February half term having been to foster parents whilst Mum was very ill. During his absence things had settled considerably and he was blamed by other children for 'spoiling things.'. Things settled again until SATs arrived, causing a lot of disruption. Despite a lot of intensive input the teacher found she was never able to give enough help. The other children were able to cope and the targeted sessions were still far better than they had been when research began, despite everything. All these outside influences made data collection and interpretation difficult. When one thinks a strategy is beginning to take effect something goes wrong for a child. So just looking at data could show poor results misleadingly since the teacher researcher has no control over outside events and maybe the particular strategy was a good one.

It was also difficult to collect evidence when circumstances demanded that two things had to be worked on concurrently, for example, with several children it was vital that the behaviour modification programmes were started whilst also trying other ideas from the Action Research cycle. It then was not possible to unravel which was having most effect.

Morling summarised her feelings by stating that she was not satisfied with the data collection and that she felt some conclusions were based on intuition. However, she considered that the support gained from several sources had made their contribution to lessening the problems experienced and made for a better environment for learning.

6. Circle Games and the Raising of Self Esteem

D. Webb (1991)

Background

As a support teacher involved with emotional and behavioural difficulties in pupils of all ages, Webb had been aware many times that solving individual problems in isolation does not work. There are a great many influences on an individual within a school and a class situation, all of which play a part in the way individuals behave. The action research decided upon was to investigate various class groupings and the use of self esteem circles. Specifically the enquiry was to look at the following: awareness of group dynamics, changes in individuals' specific behaviours, and changes in pupil/teacher relationships.

The need to look at self esteem had arisen because a vast majority of the pupils referred to him over the past four years appeared to have suffered from 'rock bottom' self-esteem. They found it difficult to like themselves and equally found it almost impossible to believe that anyone liked them at all. Another trait, apparently displayed by many, was that of accepting praise and appreciating it especially when it was given in front of others.

Action Research

Taking all the above mentioned factors into consideration, it became necessary to find an approach which dealt with the whole problem of self esteem within the group, class or school situation rather than trying to change a specific behaviour of an individual. Having read about whole school approaches, the emphasis placed on 'ethos' in the Elton Report (1989) and the growing recognition that 'good practice' did exist and should be shared, this teacher researcher began to formulate an approach which would hopefully work for the benefit of both the pupils and the staff of a school.

He started by looking back at his own teaching over the past twenty years and identified one element that was common to all classes taught. That element was drama, not just the normal drama lesson of scripts and play acting but an approach which involved group circle games. These games were specifically aimed at self esteem, group activities, oral skills, aural skills, interpersonal relationships and problem solving.

This approach was given an up-to-date relevance when an article appeared in the *Times Educational Supplement* describing the work being carried out by Jenny Mosley, an independent educational consultant working for Wiltshire Educational Authority. Her work in primary and secondary schools develops and enhances children's self esteem through the use of a technique called 'Circle-Time'.

The principles of Circling involve the issue of respect in the areas of language, listening, time, truth and equality for all participating. This involves both pupils and teachers. For many pupils the teacher is a 'significant other'. This has been described by Borba (1982) as obtaining

> when the child values the teacher as a person and when the child feels he or she is a significant being to the teacher. It is important, then, that the teacher's attitudes invite and nurture positive self-enhancement in the children he or she deals with. Since teachers' attitudes are controlled by their own feeling of competency and self-worth and by feelings about the children they are working with, it is important that teachers periodically review their own self-pictures.

Circle-Time puts all involved on an equal footing and all become more able to express their own views, to listen to each other, to work out sensible solutions to school and class problems and to feel part of a large group they enjoy and trust. Circle-Time allows the adult to become part of the whole group and be seen in a participating rather than an authoritarian role. The basic idea is that everyone has at least two sets of responsibilities: oneself and the group. Through Circle-Time, both pupils and teachers become a closer team building the group by mutual trust and respect.

Circles can be constructed to deal with specific problems or to give a universal overview of a problem, allowing teachers to target situations likely to make significant changes for the group as a whole.

The main problem with setting an action plan for such a demanding task was what aspect to target first. The teacher researcher used a technique to effect positive change in personal and group situations based upon four simple statement headings:

Where am I now?
Where do I want to be in the future?
What will hinder my progress?
What will help my progress?

When all these questions have been answered, one can then draw up an action plan in three parts:

Short Term; Medium Term; Long Term

The 'Force Field' that follows gives a basic idea of the stages that one goes through and shows that with a little honesty one can come up with a workable plan. The other, and more important aspect, is that it makes the user decide upon actions beginning with the immediate future. It also helps one to look at what is possible in actual situations and hopefully does away with the frustration of non-achievement.

Webb selected for his short term goals the construction of a basic session outline, including an observation sheet for participating staff and five session plans allowing for progression. He then chose two junior schools and similar age groups which had a class which contained a pupil referred to the LEA Disaffected Support Unit.

In the medium term he felt it important to complete five sessions with the selected classes and to evaluate the outcomes. In the longer term he wished to look at possible changes in sessions, discuss the implications for teaching style and technique, follow up the referred individuals concerned into their secondary schools, and finally to provide comprehensive training for teachers in using the 'Circle-Time' techniques.

His chosen schools had Year 6 classes in which two boys had been referred to the Support Service Unit; both having displayed similar disruptive behaviours. Part of the action research support package was working with the whole class using 'Circle-Time' to try to highlight the social group dynamics of the whole class, concentrating on the following features: working together in a team or group, listening to all members of the class or group, sharing ideas, accepting that someone else may have the right answer and, most importantly, each individual being responsible for the behaviour of the whole group.

Each session was to be forty-five minutes and contain five or six main elements. The class teachers were given the opportunity of being part of the 'circle' or observing from outside. Both chose to observe from without. The structure of the session was very prescriptive so as to allow for accurate comparison. Each class would initially have three sessions and then a decision would be made in the light of the results as to whether additional sessions would be of use.

As the pupils came in they firstly would form a circle with their chairs or by sitting on the floor. At this point Webb, as the session leader, would take no notice of behaviour or sound level. This part of the session is entitled Waiting Game. At this point the teacher must also ignore the pupils and must not intervene or reprimand any individual. The object of this game is to show them that every individual is responsible for the group's behaviour and that the session or activities within the session cannot begin until all members of the class are ready to proceed. This is usually a very frustrating time for class teachers as they feel that this is a reflection on their own management abilities. It is in fact a good indicator of group dynamics. This game is played at the beginning of every session and it is explained to the group that hopefully the settling down period will get quicker as they become more competent 'circlers'. It is useful at that time to point out that in fact the game is played at the start of all activities, and that those activities cannot proceed until all are ready to begin.

The second part is the Rule Game. This game is essential for the smooth running of the session and again would be repeated in a slightly altered form every session. Webb worked on the basis of five rules: Sensible Behaviour (SB), Sensible Language (SL), Taking Part (TP), Being Ready (BR) and Listening (L).

The abbreviations are an essential part of this game as they are written large on a sheet of paper and then the pupils are asked if they understand the rules. They, of course, do not because they do not know what the abbreviations mean. So when it is suggested that the session is started and that anyone who breaks the rules sits out of individual activities this does cause the spread of a worried look. The rules are then explained and referred to throughout the session. At the start of each session the rules are checked. Breaking the rules leads to the pupil sitting out of that particular activity; afterwards they may rejoin the circle. (It is important to ask them what feelings they experienced whilst on the outside).

The control mechanism is the circle which introduces the concept of an outside control or switch which has the job of turning on and turning off language. The objective is to teach the pupils how to recognise physical cues when they are involved in a vocal exchange.

The content of the circle must be a positive one. Therefore, the best type of circle is one dealing with favourites. Everyone has a favourite film or book, a favourite colour or meal, so it allows everyone to be heard. The initial rounds are kept to very easy going favourites but as one gets to know the pupils one can introduce such subjects as friends and relatives. Another more emotive subject is that of 'wishes'. Webb used this subject just before Christmas with a class of Year 6 pupils which unfortunately resulted in five pupils in tears, wishing for such things as a father's return home, or the resurrection of a dead grandparent. Based on this experience, wishes should only be used when one knows the pupils well and knows that they can sustain the emotional pressure.

This circle is particularly good for bringing out the quiet and the shy. It gives them a small amount of time which is all their own and no other person is going to butt in. It stops the session from being taken over by those who always use vocal muscle to get what they want.

A whole class 'brainstorm' can be used. This is a chance for the pupils to shout out ideas about a subject immediately instead of sitting in frustration with all their hands held high in space. The session leader is scribe and writes all ideas down on a large sheet of paper, every idea must be written whether sensible or otherwise. All ideas have equal importance and this allows every member of the class to feel that his or her idea will be listened to and will be valued as a contribution to the whole. The first one is usually based on such titles as Friendship, Groups, Classes etc.

In the beginning the groups are self selecting, then gradually the session leader will decide upon the group structure taking into account the class teacher's requirements. It is with these activities that one can insert a touch of humour into the proceedings, e.g. '101 things to do with a Supermarket bag'.

The final element of the session is a Truth Circle in which pupils are required to give honest answers to questions posed. Webb warns that one must be very careful with this activity otherwise all previously good work can easily be undone. The session leader must be sensitive to the emotional needs of the group and act accordingly. After a few sessions this can be one of the most rewarding elements of Circle Time, but it must be handled with extreme care!

The sessions usually ended by running through a quick review and then thanking them for their hard work and sensible behaviour.

Sometimes the teacher will give out good work stickers or certificates but Webb considers they are not really necessary as verbal praise is usually enough.

Outcomes

Having chosen very carefully the two classes that he was to work with, Webb approached both class teachers and received very favourable signals. Both teachers were well established with a long experience of primary teaching behind them. Both stated, however, that this was the first opportunity since training college that they had the chance to sit back and watch someone teach their class. This was to be the first plus of the programme. Both teachers talked afterwards of spotting individuals whom they had not considered at all in the past, and those pupils had made considerable contributions to the whole. They also spoke of the referred pupils as quiet, involved and sensible.

Each teacher was given an observation sheet with which to observe either an individual, a group or the whole class. As can be seen in Appendix 1, the session is divided into five-minute bands and the observer simply notes observations using the abbreviations provided or ones personal to them. After each session there was a chance to discuss the observations and to set the following session agenda. Because of the open feeling of the sessions and the frank exchanges between leader and class, both teachers felt at ease discussing in a very objective way the structure, the content and the results. In this way, the sessions were tailor-made, covering aspects of concern for that particular class.

At every possible juncture Webb made it very clear that the structure was a tool and could be used in many areas of the curriculum. It was not considered a success because it was a Drama session and drama sessions are just 'playing around', it was a success because the structure was thought 'sound'. The development of the structure was found dependent on the imaginative use that the teacher puts it to! Webb makes a further point stating, 'Open and truthful criticism of each other's performance was paramount; learning cannot take place where the basic facts are being covered up. If something is going wrong then there is a need for clear discussion and a use of facts. That is why I believe that credibility is so important between staff involved in such exercises.'

Appendix 2 contains the first three session plans used with the classes. They explain the format used and contain elements which are the basic building blocks for success.

Conclusions

A major problem with a study of this nature is that time is very limited and the flow of sessions is sometimes interrupted due to the nature of support work. Neither group had a continuous flow of sessions, so the effect of large time spans had to be taken into consideration.

Webb indicated a further problem which was that there was no time to set up class teacher led sessions so as to create a balanced, objective view. Neither was there time for the staff involved to try out the technique during a longer time span, maybe even on a daily basis. As an action research study 'Circling' offers an interesting tool in achieving more self-disciplined and thoughtful pupils and staff and can produce dramatic changes in the ethos of schools and classrooms. Both pupils and staff show each other more respect, there is a feeling of belonging, a feeling of mutual support when demands begin to mount and the return of an element of good 'old fashioned' fun.

Being respectful, listening, sharing problems, sharing discovery with others (especially self-discovery), solving problems together as a whole group and realising that others may have a different answer – these were all very positive aspects to emerge during this action research. All are vitally important in the building of a group, class and school ethos. Most pupils like to be noticed and to be valued and the use of 'Circle Time' can allow this process to be developed in a positive way.

Whole School Policies for Integrating Pupils with Special Educational Needs

The whole school approach, it can be argued, has perhaps caused most difficulties in the secondary school as a result of the attempt to adopt the guidelines of the Warnock Report (1978). For historically, the secondary school has produced more didactic, teacher centred teaching with an emphasis on a class learning skills and there has been a greater tendency to group pupils by ability than in the primary schools.

It is therefore of particular interest that the projects described in this section have all been undertaken by secondary school staff. Ensor (1989) concentrated on the perceptions of pupils where a whole school approach had been adopted. Copestake (1990) focused his action research on a scheme to aid the development of learning material whilst Coe and Alger (1991) outline the planning for a change of teaching strategy. Basell (1989) concludes this section by describing the early stages of a study focusing on special needs of bilingual pupils.

7. Developing an Integrated Support System

T. Ensor (1989)

Background

In this project, Ensor concentrated on the feelings of pupils in his school. He chose to investigate more fully a small group of Year 9 pupils who had exhibited learning difficulties. They had been taught together in the early part of their secondary schooling and were to be integrated as fully as possible into the subject teaching areas in Year 10.

Action Research

This teacher researcher expressed some doubts about the system that this class would be facing both in practical and philosophical terms. He outlined the organisation of the teaching of English and Maths by stating:

> The English department created a 'bottom' set in the Years 10 and 11. The support department assisted in the creation of this set and supplied a teacher for it. The number in this class was kept deliberately small (10 – 15).

This went against his overall philosophy but it was recognised as a pragmatic decision. If all the children who need support were distributed to the other four mixed-ability groups, then the task of consistent supporting would prove impracticable. The Mathematics department employed strict setting from top to bottom. In this case it proved impossible to supply a 'bottom' set teacher. There were certain factors which persuaded him to accept this situation. These were: the assurance that children in need would receive consistent support; the Mathematics and English teachers being happiest with this arrangement; the well-being of support teachers who had faced numerous changes in a short time; the continuity of relationship between students and support teachers and the overall welfare of the children.

With these identified groups in place, he stated 'I was happier to accept the wide spread of these pupils amongst the option subjects. Those children identified for the investigation spend the rest of their time in mixed-ability groups.'

The aim of this project was to interview this group of pupils and by using open ended, semi-structured questions to elicit their feelings about this development. His purpose was to help the former members of this class to 'open up'. To this end he stated his questions were 'of a general nature and as open-ended as possible to allow them to state their views.'

Outcomes

In general, the pupils interviewed were positive about the changes that had been made: 'all the students expressed a feeling of being more comfortable socially, although those with less confidence more readily expressed a desire for extra help with their lessons.'

Student A was quite adamant in his summing up of his new situation.

'You feel like you've got an equal opportunity with everybody in a big class – it's better. I didn't like being in that class at all – he's in a special class - so he's a div.'

Student B felt that: 'The lessons are just the same ... but they don't pick on you now.'

Student D was less confident: 'You're given daggers an' that from other classes (when you've done something wrong, made a mistake). It happens a lot in Maths – it's hard Maths.'

Student E, in response to a question as to whether or not he felt he stood out more in his third year, reflected: 'They could call me 'remmy', but not much.' However he said this had never happened in his present school year.

During interviews the students became more confident yet it was clear that areas of worry coincided with particular lessons.

Student A: 'I'd like to have a couple of reading lessons like I used to.'

Student B: 'Maths is a lot harder; last year they used to teach us a lot more!'

Student D: 'I'd like to change it (the overall situation) to more reading lessons.'

The responses to the questions about support were confused and unsure. To be blunt, these students did not really understand what the support teachers were doing, generally perceiving that the whole group (or the subject teacher) was being supported. Ensor found it hard to explain that the support teachers were there by design.

Student A: 'I'd rather ask the proper Science teacher myself.'

Student C: 'I just wait for the (subject) teacher to come – they give you help sometimes.'

Student F: 'He helps the whole class.'

Many of the responses displayed a degree of immaturity; students often refused to ask for help within a mixed ability class as it constituted an admission of failure. Ensor produced a list of areas and issues for future attention. These included feelings that the students were less exposed and more comfortable in larger mixed-ability groups, and that they felt the need for more direct contact related to specific areas of difficulty. Importantly, they were not aware of the individual identification and attention practised by the support teachers and in some cases actively discouraged or ignored it. Further, the students were finding friendship groupings more flexible and easier to form and maintain.

Conclusions

Ensor states:
'My research has only recently been completed. I have brought the preceding interpretation to the attention of the department and it will form the basis of the future agendas. I was concerned, however, that we made some kind of immediate response. In some way, I felt that this was a necessity. I had been quite moved by the depth of feeling expressed by the students and in short felt rather guilty that there was a danger that we might lose those deep, meaningful relationships that we like to think are our stock in trade. I turned to a colleague from another school who was good enough to take time to listen to my interpretation of the data and suggest practical moves we might make. Given the finite resource (of available support) previously described, I was wrestling with the inherent contradictions apparent in some of the points which had been made. I decided to take my peer group (the network's) advice and try to institute direct contact lessons in that (sometimes) dead time between morning registration and first lesson (25 minutes). The support teacher who had returned on a half timetable had not been assigned to a tutor group and was ideal to use in setting up this kind of contact. I discussed the matter with the deputy headteacher responsible and he was enthusiastic. I suggested that we start the scheme as a pilot study with a view to involving more teachers in the future. We also discussed the possibility of crediting those involved teachers with "contact" time during these lessons, which would have an influence on the number of times they are called to "cover" absent colleagues.

The school had already set precedents by arranging "early" language lessons. It was prudent to wait until we set next year's timetable priorities before putting the scheme on a more formal footing, although we agreed that the teacher concerned would not be called for registration cover during these "contact" periods (three mornings per week).

An evaluation will have to be made on this particular experiment, but I had the feeling that the students should be involved in its inception. Consequently I arranged to talk to all of the "bottom" English set (all interviewees are in this set). With the permission of the interviewees I gave the whole class a brief resume of our findings. I suggested that others in the group might share the same feelings and wish to be considered for the 'contact' lessons. I did not ask for responses there and then but made myself available after the lesson, so they could come and see me on an individual basis. All thirteen pupils came to see me either singly or in twos and threes; furthermore they were able to identify the areas in which they felt they needed help. The process continues; we are now matching times and areas of difficulty. Ideally I wanted a paired reading 1 : 1 approach, but this is not immediately possible and the overriding factor is one of being seen to respond in the eyes (and hearts) of the pupils.'

8. Preparation of Learning Materials for SEN Pupils by Mainstream Teachers

B. Copestake (1990)

Background

For the past four years, special needs provision has moved consistently towards meeting special needs in the mainstream classroom with subject teachers being supported by a hierarchy of provision beginning with subject (SEN) liaison teachers and continuing through personal and social development (PSD), learning and counselling support before the involvement of outside agencies. The emphasis has been on making the mainstream curriculum more accessible to children with learning difficulties through differentiated learning tasks and an increasing awareness of the cross-curricular nature of the development of reading, spelling and writing skills. Copestake argued that the increasing involvement of mainstream staff in the examination and revision of their own learning tasks was a natural progression of this policy and the INSET programme that supported it.

To accommodate this development in a formal structure, the school allocated 100 teaching periods per week to special needs. This allocation included the timetables of SEN department staff (1.5 teachers) and twelve periods of time allocated to the school counsellor. The rest of the time was available because of temporary over-staffing and in addition to being used for the project discussed below was used to create 'extra' teaching groups in some subjects in the upper school.

Following discussions between the head of learning support and the Headteacher it was decided to 'free' staff from the timetable for the preparation of learning tasks for SEN pupils.

Action Research

The preparation for the project included the following strategies:

- The whole staff had been involved in INSET concerning the whole-school contribution to the reading curriculum and the nature of the reading process.

- Subject SEN Liaison Teachers had been involved in two half days of INSET dealing with identifying pupils with special needs and assessing and matching pupil capabilities and learning task demands.

- The equivalent of one day of the two INSET Days at the beginning of the Autumn Term was devoted to an examination of readability, the need to match pupil capability and learning task demands and the simplification of learning materials. Following this each member of staff had been given a booklet on 'Readability and The Simplification of Learning Materials' which was to form part of their SEN Handbook.

- Staff involved in the Learning Materials project met together to discuss the project and then were given time to allocate responsibilities and identify targets for action on the second INSET Day.

Outcomes

Despite one or two problems with staff 'losing' their SEN time to cover in the first two weeks of the year, the system of allocating time generally worked smoothly. Supporting the staff proved to be a big problem for the head of learning support. For the first half of the Autumn Term every spare moment was spent talking to staff and recording what they were doing.

The system of taking time off the SEN teachers to 'buy' time for the project had reduced the amount of time available for direct contact with SEN pupils to only 15 periods for the whole school. This and the fact that the new first year intake was proving to have more than its fair share of special needs meant that progress in other areas of departmental work was being sacrificed to an unacceptable degree. The amount of time allocated by the head of learning support to staff on the Learning Materials Project had to be severely curtailed in the second half of the Autumn Term. This was unsatisfactory as it was clear that regular contact with the supporting teacher was necessary to maintain the momentum of the project.

During the first half of the second term the head of learning support was able to allocate a little more time to discuss work with individual teachers but it was impossible to see all 15 staff frequently enough. As a result he organised a series of meetings after school — meeting each department involved in turn. This proved useful and allowed some discussion between staff involved which had not been possible beforehand. The situation was also eased at the end of the Spring Term by the use of INSET funds to release the Head of Learning Support from 'cover' responsibilities for enough time to see all 15 staff for 35 minutes each (one teaching period).

From the beginning it was intended that subject staff should identify their own areas of action which reflected the needs of the pupils in their subject areas. Little direction, therefore, was given initially so as not to inhibit this subject orientated approach. Some staff had difficulty in identifying possible targets for action and there was some delay before starting.

Conclusions

It was accepted from the outset that the project would be seen as part of the SEN staff development programme and that any enhancement of experience of staff would be as valuable an end product as hard copy learning materials.

Most teachers focused on the need to simplify written tasks so that the work was accessible to all pupils. In three cases this resulted in genuinely differentiated tasks when existing work was analysed and alternatives produced with particular children in mind. In other cases, the approach was to produce work that could be done by all the pupils in mixed ability groups. Sometimes there was an element of differentiation by providing extension tasks for the more able.

Of the staff who worked on learning materials in this way several were in fact having to produce learning materials for the first time — that is to say there was not an existing set of materials or tasks to modify or adapt. In some cases there was no scheme of work available either.

Simplification largely centred on the language of written worksheets or information sheets that had been teacher produced. For example, technical vocabulary was eliminated or introduced in a more supported manner.

In several cases staff were satisfied that the learning materials in use were already as simple as could be and could not be simplified further. There was in some cases a reluctance to attempt to modify learning situations for one or two pupils or for one year only.

An important development from this initiative was that one member of staff arranged for an end of unit test to be read to an individual pupil and noted the (vastly improved) result. Beyond that, one member of staff devised a set of cards to be used independently of the existing scheme of work that drew attention to the visual analysis of the written names of items of equipment and measurement used in the subject. Another recorded a class reading book onto cassettes as an aid to pupils unable to read the book independently for themselves.

There had been, therefore, a diversity of response with the work done during this time reflecting not only the personality and approach of the individual teacher but the nature of the subject and its departmental organisation. Meanwhile, with the project having approximately one third of its allocated time to run, plans were made for evaluating its impact through a future network.

9. An Initiative with Teachers of Year Seven Pupils

D. Coe and M. Alger (1991)

Background

These teacher researchers undertook a fundamental review of the processes of learning and teaching strategies in their school in order to provide, within their school, an outline model for the staff which would allow them to provide for every child access to the skills, knowledge and understanding provided by the National Curriculum. This initially took the form of staff discussions to introduce this process and set up a system of co-ordinated classroom observations concentrating on teaching style and class management.

Within a school many forces are at work, the plan therefore had to take this into account. Further, teaching is an individual, even a lonely, occupation which of necessity often requires the individual to confront the problems face to face behind the closed doors of the classroom. Implicit in that situation is the misguided idea that an inability to 'control' all circumstances is a reflection on the 'professionalism' of the teacher concerned. It was therefore important to get the members of staff to realise that any selected form of classroom observation with the purpose of improving the opportunity for learning was not in any way appraisal of them as individuals.

Much reading and hours of discussion led to the conclusion that it was an impossible task without the whole hearted support and involvement of the staff at every level. To do this the staff had to be given the power of veto and be actively involved at each and every level. They needed to be able to openly disagree with any action without fear of hostility and have the platform to put forward their own suggestions without hindrance.

To achieve any change therefore, it quickly became clear that the project would take time, discussion and tact.

Action Research

First it was decided to put out a discussion document outlining the main points that it was felt were essential to any worthwhile programme within the school. This was given to each member of staff and the contents explained. The departments were then asked to discuss this as part of their regular departmental meetings and any fundamental differences of opinion or objections were invited. The document was at the same time considered by the senior management team and also a special meeting of the academic committee was devoted to considering its aims, objectives and suggestions.

From these discussions the following points emerged:

- A seven point scale of lesson assessment of the staff should be adopted. It was essential that any in-house based assessment must be a fair system which gave every individual on the teaching staff the opportunity to indicate their views.

- The grouping of the pupils should be looked at. It was felt that this factor would play a large part in any classroom management situation.

- The effective use of resources would act as a 'marker' and highlight areas of need not noticed by those normally outside that area of concern.

- Classroom management was emphasised because it was felt that this may have a great deal of relevance to the teaching and learning situation for particular teachers.

- The opportunity to include a layout of the classroom was also held to be important as an incentive to those taking part to look closely at the positioning of the desks within the rooms and encouraging discussion as to the appropriateness of this layout with the pupils whom they were teaching.

- The inclusion of a section on classroom display which would highlight the importance and appropriateness of such material.

An INSET day was used to further the discussion of the best way forward with all staff. It was decided in advance that a checklist of appropriate topics for classroom observations would have to be constructed. In order to initiate these discussions a questionnaire was circulated to all staff. This was done not only to provide a body of information but also to act as an outline agenda for the day.

For the day itself there needed to be clearly defined rules and a reiteration of the central statements and concepts in order to hope to achieve any degree of success. To this end, all members of the senior management team had inputs into the day's proceedings.

It was felt important to get the participants to understand the terms that were to be used. One of the main thrusts was to highlight the main teaching and learning styles, such as Passive and Active: What are they? What do they entail? How do they differ from each other? These may appear to be obvious questions to those who have been involved in this area. But the discussions and plenary sessions embarked upon throughout the action research stopped colleagues from falling into the trap of assumption. Basically it was pointed out that in teaching we use both passive and active teaching styles, depending on the messages and material we wish to use. Passive is the style that has almost no input from the pupils, whereas the active is when the teacher is a facilitator who helps and advises as and when required.

The problem was firstly how to introduce the tasks to be undertaken that session. Using background information and giving definitions to the areas to be discussed was considered vital but how to get the staff involved was the main challenge. No amount of facilitating or discussion can detract from the fact that work has to take place and tasks be completed. It was decided to approach this by posing a series of questions displayed on an overhead projector which it was hoped would encourage responses initially from the floor and then from departments in their sessions.

The returned responses from the departments in the form of questionnaires were both thoughtful and constructive. In every case the members of staff had shown a strong commitment to the tasks and reviewed the check lists professionally.

The later presentations by the departments indicated a great number of areas that needed to be reconstructed but in every case the suggestions were listened to by all the staff and then general questions were invited by that department to see if any consensus could be reached. Within the structure of the day, although a great deal of departmental discussion and input took place the feedback was necessarily restricted. This meant having to gain the approval of colleagues to construct a check list after attempting to get a consensus from the returns.

Certain immediate changes to the proposals were obvious because a strong consensus was clearly indicated. These were:

- The observed staff member must also have a sheet on which they can indicate their feelings on the performance and environment. This it was felt would also give the opportunity to look at both points of view and may give further evidence that might be of help. It also gave the observed 'the right of reply' if areas of complete difference were indicated.

- The observers ought to be departmental rather than the head or deputy. This was not unexpected and the initial inclusion of those colleagues in the original document was intended in order for departments to 'look within' as a positive move forward in their affairs.

- The seven point scale, although initially coming from the departmental heads' meetings and the discussions, was rejected by the majority of the discussion groups in favour of a five point scale.

A number of other points were raised by the participating staff. These included the question of assessment in the National Curriculum programme, pupil profiles, support available for pupils with special educational needs and the training needs of the staff in the school.

Outcomes

The INSET day was an enormous success. All the targets which had been set were achieved and a great deal more besides. All that now remained for this stage was to digest the gathered information and develop the check list for classroom observation that all staff had a part in making.

The sorting, collating and selection of the final sections of the check list from the departments' returns was not as difficult a task as it first seemed for they suggested remarkably similar approaches. Certain ideas were of immediate benefit and indicated procedures that had been overlooked. For example, the idea of breaking the lesson down into three parts, i.e. Introduction, Activity and Application. This gave further possible material for analysis because one could see how the approach was either adapted or the surroundings changed. (See Appendix 3).

There was one area however, where the action researchers as organisers took the decision. As indicated above, the consensus indicated a five point scale. However, it was decided that a four point scale would be far more beneficial. This was born from experience that when confronted with a scale system that allows a middle choice, especially when others were also observing, the tendency would be to choose the middle option.

The observation check list was finally produced and issued to each department for their comments. Special timetabled meetings discussed the form that the check list had taken and the actual tasks to be conducted by each and every department. It was at these meetings that the differences that appeared on the check list were explained and it was indicated that one lesson from each of the year groups needed to be observed as a test of the proposed observation check list. This had to be done because this was an attempt to begin a whole school approach to the issue. This it was felt had begun to be achieved and could not be allowed to drift away and not become an important aspect of the school's structure.

The initial observations were encouraging and the results indicated interesting areas that could be further explored. The process continued and at the time of this report reached the second phase whereby feedback was given in timetabled meetings where further areas of development that have come to light through the individual check list could be explored. For example, does the department have poor displays because of its attitude to the material or are there financial implications? The check list was intended to be treated as a two way medium; the vehicle by which objective observation can take place and constructive development emerge. It also provided a means by which departments clearly indicate their areas of need with statistical evidence in order to explain and justify budget distributions.

Conclusions

The researchers summarised their experience in the following terms: 'The project became bigger and bigger. The process that had to go through in the setting up and developing of the action research were invaluable. The reading that had to accompany the study did increase our understanding of the nature of the task we had set ourselves but it did not indicate the depth to which we still have to go if any lasting success is to follow.'

The last statement is without doubt one that all future action researchers need to keep in mind if they wish their research to be practical and beneficial. It must be progressive, developmental and be workable for both staff and pupils and have support in the school.

10. Bilingual Pupils in 'Normal' Lessons

J. Basell (1989)

Background

Basell concentrated her evaluation on the preparations for supporting bilingual pupils in a secondary school. These pupils had already gained a good command of English.

Her concern was to find out what the bilingual child was getting out of 'normal' lessons. Was it what the teacher thought? Were there any unsuspected difficulties, or indeed benefits, to be uncovered?

She pointed out there were a number of stereotypical ideas on bilingual children and their achievements which had been mentioned on INSET courses and at teachers' meetings and conferences which she attended since joining the Bilingual Support Service. For example, bilingual children were assumed to:

- underachieve nationally;
- have poor examination results;
- be often in the SEN or remedial classes.

Asian pupils in particular were believed to be hard working, conscientious, and well behaved.

Further, she felt that these stereotypes implying that Asian, including Chinese children 'keep a low profile' and are 'no trouble', indicated in the mind of some teachers an important degree of success. However, she considered that in reality this is not so. Firstly, these pupils are just as likely to underachieve nationally and have poor examination results. Secondly, in real terms this form of social compliance cannot be regarded as any form of academic success.

Her experience of working with such groups of pupils is that they were a 'regular bunch of school kids' – some in exam classes working hard while others have been described by their teachers as 'average', others 'naughty'. Some clearly had no need of extra language tuition while others needed the support of the special needs department staff in their schools.

Action Research

Discussion with colleagues in the network and in schools resulted in deciding to shadow a class for the equivalent of a school day, to interview the teachers before the day, and the pupils fairly soon after the lessons.

It was considered that not fewer than two and not more than four children would be an ideal number for what was really to be a pilot study, and that non-bilingual pupil should be included in the group.

Once the topic of the research had been decided the problems associated with it were much more clear. They included the following:

- To get the idea approved by senior management colleagues.
- To obtain the co-operation of the teachers, and of the children.
- How to timetable the shadowing?
- Production of non-intimidating question prompts for pupil interviews.
- Time for shadowing and liaison (limited by not always being in the school).
- Approval of relevant school committee.
- Loan of tape-recorder and tape.
- Location of suitable 'interview' room.
- Finding suitable time for pupil interviews.

Outcomes

An unsuspected problem was approval of the heads of departments and representatives of the pastoral care staff who serve on the school curriculum and staff development committee which has a sub-committee of senior staff. After consideration, this sub-committee asked that the project be postponed until later in the year when it would fit into a whole staff initiative which was being planned. This staff initiative was aimed at tracking children through the school to find out what variety of experiences the children were having in their training situations and whether curriculum change was necessary. Further, if this was the case, how this should be implemented. Whilst this appeared to be somewhat different from, but compatible with the aims of the action research proposed, the researcher was nevertheless asked to attend the next full meeting of the committee when the whole school initiative was to be discussed.

Conclusions

Although this was not envisaged as an easy piece of research, there turned out to be more planning and liaison necessary than was first realised. However, all the ground work was now complete.

When the in-school staff development initiative got under way later in the year, it was hoped that it would be possible to complete this piece of action research at the same time when the selection of the pupils, the timetabling of the shadowing, and the analysis and interpretation of data received could be carried out.

Medical Problems

Medical problems can be a fundamental cause of difficulty for pupils with special educational needs. Male and Thompson (1985) have suggested that more and more pupils with complex medical problems are likely to be found in the mainstream school. It is hardly surprising therefore, that some participants in these Networks have taken such issues for their line of enquiry.

The studies presented in the following section illustrate some of the problems that can be exhibited and also the variety of schools where such problems occur. Shutes (1988) for example worked in a special school and illustrates how an action research programme helped a severely handicapped girl. Simpson (1990) concentrated her work on a boy in her first year at infant school with dyspraxia, while Spolton (1988) looked at how diabetes may have caused difficulties in the learning development of a child in a mainstream junior school.

11. Improving Problems of Balance for a Nursery Age Child

V. Shutes (1988)

Background

This teacher researcher worked at a Special School. She described it as a school for children with severe learning difficulties where she was based in the Nursery with a class of eight children, four of whom were profoundly handicapped both physically and mentally. The remaining four were mobile. This study was concerned with one of the profoundly handicapped children.

The specific area chosen to research was a gross motor problem. This was because 50 per cent of this group of children had this or a similar problem. Further, the other children entering the Nursery at a later date may also be similarly affected and therefore require work in that area.

S was chosen for a variety of reasons — there were so many problems that could have been tackled that selecting one and narrowing it down was a problem in itself. However, S's difficulties were highlighted by a visit to school from her foster mother. In essence, S's foster mother was very petite whilst her natural mother was tall. Although S was only three years old, she was big for her age and because of this, the foster mother was already finding it difficult to cope with the lifting and carrying involved in daily routines and would obviously find this more difficult as time went on. This visit really prompted the teacher researcher to use S in her action research as she felt the foster mother was feeling 'low' and to have this special programme especially if it was at all successful, would give her and the rest of the family a psychological boost.

S had attended school only a short time. To begin with, this was on a part-time basis — three days a week. This was because travelling from where she lived to school is some 20 miles and this made the days long and tiring. It was felt initially that this would be all she could cope with. During the school day, S had a broadly based curriculum consisting of language/communication skills, cognitive physiotherapy, fine motor skills, creative and musical skills, and a sensory stimulation programme. She worked on her own individual programme on a daily basis.

S was a microcephalic and also suffered from epilepsy. She had approximately one grand-mal fit per week and was on daily medication. She attended hospital regularly and her general health was good. She was a pretty child with dark curly hair and beautiful brown eyes. Her parents felt strongly that if at all possible they would like her to eventually walk. However, at that time she could only balance for a few seconds sitting; walking was in the future.

Physiotherapy played a very important part in S's day. She had a daily general physio session consisting of various passive movements, head control, balancing, ball work. She also had hydrotherapy every third week, splash pool sessions weekly and ball pool sessions two or three times a week. Her physio programme was devised by her own physiotherapist, who came to school weekly to visit her and if she was not in school, she made regular home visits. The physiotherapist agreed that in the long term, walking (perhaps with aids) could be achieved.

S was also on a feeding programme — again assisted by the physiotherapist and occupational therapist who between them suggested suitable seating arrangements with the speech therapist. S ate a minced diet and drank from a cup with two handles. She had poor chewing action and was fed by an adult, using a plastic spoon and placing food in the side of her mouth. She could hold her own cup, in one or two hands (depending on her mood) and although to begin with 'hooked' her thumbs through the handles, latterly she had gripped the handles firmly.

When S first started school, she was doubly incontinent but on a habit based programme for toileting had improved tremendously. From wearing nappies at all times, she latterly wore them for travelling to and from school and at night − but wore panties all through the day.

S had severe developmental delay in all areas. She had reasonably good head control − she could lift it on verbal request, and obviously this continued to need a lot of work to enable her to balance successfully.

S could roll from side to side, not on request but had no other movements. She sucked her fingers continuously if allowed and curled up into the foetal position. To prevent this, she wore elbow gaiters. She had no language as such but made pleasure sounds when she was happy and grumbles when displeased.

She had electrical hearing tests and her hearing was reported to be normal. She responded to sounds by body movements, eye movements and turning her head − but she was often too slow to respond to the voice. She was startled by loud noises and responded particularly well to music. She had been seen by the ophthalmologist and had healthy eyes. She did however have some damage to the visual centre in the brain. There had been a terrific impiovement in eye contact since attending school and it was now firmly established.

This general profile on S provided an insight into the child as a whole and showed the various areas that were being worked on. The improvement in balancing that was the core of the action research was just a small part of her daily programme, albeit a very important one. It had to be remembered that S was only three years old and as such was very young to be in full time education and coping with high input in the various areas of her programme.

Action Research

Basically the plan of action for S was to concentrate solely on balancing with a view to her eventually sitting, completely unaided. This was to be achieved by an extra daily physio session of between ten and fifteen minutes. Her usual daily programme consisted of:

- supine, with passive movements to all limbs;
- prone: bridging and rolling exercises, with wedge to encourage head support and the use of Skooter board (with arms support);
- two and four point kneeling exercises sitting, cross legged, straight legged and side sitting;
- standing exercises using Flexistand and Piedro Boots.

For the action research, a further ten to fifteen minutes daily on the various sitting positions, using trial and error to find the most suitable sitting position was to be introduced.

In this project, S had a full week of daily sessions before the half term holiday — she then intended to have another 5 weeks of concentrated effort, but unfortunately one week was completely lost due to S's illness and various other days were lost due to Makaton/Portage courses and general classroom pressure. Out of 30 sessions 21 were held and on some of those, S was not on top form.

Because of the input from the physiotherapist, the programme was often slightly different each week — depending on how she had responded and any modifications that seemed feasible. This extract from the teacher's diary indicated how the programme developed.

Week 1

I worked sitting behind S with both of us facing the large mirror. This was a good situation for positioning but S tended to throw herself backwards, knowing that I was there and could catch her.

Week 2

I sat in front of S. I found this position awkward and although S didn't throw herself backwards as forcefully — she still went over backwards on a number of occasions.

Week 3

Non-starter — S was absent from school for 2 days and lethargic and generally unwell the remaining three. There was no point in pursuing any programmes whilst S was in this state.

Week 4

Introduced the Niagara Vibrator — as a reward for S. She appeared to like the feel of her hands on the machine. Originally, the physio and myself were going to use it by giving bursts of power whenever S was bearing weight through her arms, but eventually we left it running to keep S's hands in the correct position. There was some noticeable improvement in the lengths of balancing.

Week 5

Used the vibrator to sit on rather than have hands resting on. New balance position using ladder back chair for back support but no sideways support at all. S used her feet and legs to correct her balance and her hands were touching/gripping the side of the vibrator.

Week 6

I was out three days but the last two days there was dramatic improvement. Two minutes plus balancing in some positions.

Outcomes

The action plan worked to a certain extent. For a problem like S's, the concentrated work needs to be on-going for years rather than weeks for the full benefit to be felt. Too many days were lost due to unforeseen circumstances that in a short programme took a large percentage of the work time away. Over a longer period of time, the lost time could be made up and a better routine established. Also the pressure to do well would be reduced causing less tension all round.

Of all the data collected on S, her balancing times certainly improved from the one to two seconds initially to two minutes plus in various positions. Her head control also improved and this in turn helped eye contact — becoming easier to establish and maintain, thus showing that not just one area was improving but the child as a whole was benefiting from the structured approach of the action research. It also became apparent as the programme was implemented that S worked better first thing in the morning. In a young child this was probably quite obvious but unfortunately, in a nursery with eight young children, it was impossible to work with everyone first thing in the morning, so she had to take her turn with the rest.

The use of the vibrator as an aid was also an important factor. This was introduced at the beginning of the fourth week and it was from this time that the improvement really began. S thoroughly enjoyed the sensation and would bear weight better when it was on. She would regularly sit, unaided, whilst the vibrator was on, but topple over a few seconds after it had been switched off. This showed that as an aid the vibrator itself was important and could be used effectively to help children like her.

During the action research programme, the physiotherapist made regular visits and on the whole was pleased with S's progress. She did stress though that the balancing programme must be implemented as well as the normal physio programme, and not instead of it, because it was very important to keep up the exercises for the whole body and not just to concentrate on one area.

Conclusions

It had been both interesting and rewarding working with S on this programme. The teacher researcher and subject both had fun and the extra time spent together helped build up a good relationship between them.

Whilst S was working with the action research programme, the foster mother was also involved. She made regular visits to school as part of a home/school teaching programme within the school and during these times the opportunity would be taken to work with S, showing how she was gradually improving. This helped the foster mother who felt that S was getting a lot of input; also she realised that what she had said initially about S sitting and walking had been heard and acted upon and that the school was trying to help her in a way that was important not just to S but to S's family as a whole.

After the programme was completed, the foster mother, at her own request, continued with the balancing programme (she borrowed the vibrator and wedge from school) on a daily basis at home. She kept a detailed record and her results were pretty similar to what had been happening in school. This liaison between home and school was apparent before the action research. But it was thought that it helped cement an exceptionally good bond between the foster parent and teacher researcher, and if for no other reason, suggested that the action research had been very worthwhile.

After completion of the programme S sat for one and a half minutes on the ladder back chair, with only the back of the chair for support. she corrected herself when she began to tilt to one side by weight bearing through her arms and also her legs. This was very gratifying and although the programme won't be continued, sitting in this specific position will be.

12. Dyspraxia – An Attempt at School Based Intervention

M. Simpson (1990

Background

The problem that first presented itself was one of behaviour. M was four years old, very wild and impulsive. He scattered sand and other materials, knocked crayons on the floor and was often found fighting A, an old adversary from playschool. He was, however, always cheerful and did not appear to resent being corrected, though prone to deny anything of which he was accused. He could not really be described as disaffected, though later on he showed signs of enjoying the exasperation of adults at yet another upturned paintpot. He had an unfortunate habit of throwing sand, small toys etc, across the classroom. He was also seen tipping a large box of cars on the floor to avoid a class discussion and showing of work. While the teacher researcher took every opportunity to praise and encourage him individually, some of the other children were well aware that his writing and drawing were poor and at this stage were capable of being very scathing.

Her concern first registered when she found M sitting in the playground surrounded by a ring of menacing four-year olds. The other Reception teacher told of another occasion when he had run to her for protection. A and his friends had taken his shoe and run away with it.

More detailed observation of M's behaviour revealed that he would run up to other children (and the teacher on occasion) and cannon into them. He would also attempt to express affection by flinging his arm round other children's necks. They would retaliate or rebuff him. A space would automatically form around him when the children came to sit on the mat, as he was apt to roll about and flail his legs and arms. He was fidgety and restless when working at a table and avoided manipulative toys.

His self help skills – dressing, toileting (but not eating) were reasonably good. (The teacher researcher was later to find that his mother had some expertise in this area as she had been working with elderly people.) He had some insight into his problems. When his mother enquired if he had been a good boy that day, he said 'Yes, A was away'.

It was becoming apparent as M began to learn hand writing and to use the computer keyboard, that his fine motor control was poor. He was able to match letters and words and recognise and remember flashcards reasonably well but needed to sit with an adult as he very quickly got bored and wanted to roam round the room. M was right handed but had a bizarre pencil grip, using his whole hand, reversed with thumb down. He was given a triangular slip-on for his pencil to encourage the correct tripod hold but constantly reverted. One further factor that gave rise to concern was M's habit of pretending to fall on the floor and laugh uproariously. He was already becoming the 'Class Scapegoat'.

When M's mother was consulted, she remarked 'I don't know where it comes from. His father and I are both quiet'. She also revealed that he had been premature and was an only child of older parents. She began to come in on her half day to help in the classroom and watch M's interaction with his peers.

A review of recent research revealed quite a lot of interest in the problem of the 'Clumsy Child'. This is now a somewhat outdated term. 'Movement Difficulties' is now the favoured term as 'Clumsy' is thought to be pejorative and 'Dyspraxia' has connotations of disease.

The prognosis is usually good as it more often shows as a developmental lag than a permanent handicap. It is associated with premature and full-term, low birth weight children as well as children who have had some 'affront' to the nervous system – e.g. German Measles, febrile convulsions, encephalitis, etc. It also 'runs in some families' so such cases will represent the lower end of the genetic spectrum of motor ability.

Some of the children are very timid and withdrawn and others impulsive and foolhardy. It can be associated with an inability to keep still or – less often – with extreme inactivity. There is a correlation with low academic ability but it is sometimes found in children of high intelligence. Typically such children perform well on the W.I.S.C. Verbal, but not on the Performance scales (Nash Wortham). It can then be categorised as a specific learning disability. Poor short term memory is also commonly found.

The condition can be defined as an inability to form skilled purposive movements. There is often poor muscle tone leading to odd postures. It was interesting to learn of the importance of shoulder girdle stability in learning to write, and that it was improvable. Some children adopt very strange positions and even climb onto the desk when attempting to write. There is also often additional non-purposive movement in performing a difficult task. All teachers will be familiar with the gangling, rather eccentric individual with 'arms and legs all over the place' who might be quite intellectually able. Habits affecting social relationships – bumping into people or standing too close and invading 'personal space', are associated with the poor spatial ability which is later a handicap in spacing letters and words, general page layout, and copying from a blackboard. Temporal difficulties as in clapping rhythms and syllables have a surprising relevance to developing fluent reading.

The most significant factor was its association with behaviour difficulties. There must be much frustration particularly when such children are constantly castigated for carelessness and untidiness in their work. They are at much greater risk of being bullied and even of developing psychiatric disorder. According to some accounts, identification of movement difficulties at seven years can be predictive of this in later life. Even a mild degree of difficulty can have an effect out of all proportion on a child's self image and behaviour. Sociometric mapping studies have shown both by peer group and teacher ratings that these children are seen as unpopular. There is much prestige attached to physical prowess in the school pecking order. Many teachers will recognise the child who is inept at games, perhaps overweight, and the butt of all the jokes. P.E. tends to be an ordeal as such children are often slower in changing or late for lessons.

They may seek refuge in the corners of playgrounds since playgrounds are often perceived as places of danger and worry. The concern with inactive, physically timid, 'loner' children is that their difficulties might be overlooked as a result of their tendencies to have such low profiles.

The teacher researcher also made the point that the 'poor eater' who is the cause of so much anxiety to mothers of children starting school dinners, might be experiencing difficulty manipulating cutlery, opening crisp bags, taking tops off yoghurt pots, etc.

Action Research

There was no standardised test of physical development easily available. From descriptions in the literature a 'gross motor' test such as T.O.M.I. or P.M.A.T. would be difficult and time-consuming to apply in the classroom, and also need specialised equipment. T.O.M.I. was only scaled from five to six years up, while these children were four years. Bender Gestalt needed specialised skills to score and was not entirely relevant. At this stage the network co-ordinator advised getting in touch with the Schools Psychological Service and they came to the school for observations, and later did a full assessment. A subsequent day conference enabled the teacher researcher to extract a checklist which would be suitable for use in the classroom.

M was noticeably poor on nearly all the checklist items and several other children showed up as having less marked difficulties. A 'tramline' test (pencil line between two parallel lines with increasing angular difficulties) was conducted, and scored for the whole class as it was felt it might be useful later on in the investigation. At this time some behaviour sampling was conducted recording how many times interventions were necessary.

The physiologist's report revealed that M's head was still out of proportion with his body and he had adopted a forward leaning gait which affected his balance and ability to stop. He also had poor proprioceptive and kinaesthetic development and needed to be able to see where his limbs were before he could accomplish certain tasks. His problems were not as severe as in most of the children who were referred for remedial treatment. However, bearing in mind the difficulties his problems were causing in his social relations, the school psychologists supplied several suggestions for a remedial programme which could be undertaken in school. It was suggested that his mother might also like to work with him at home.

Children with these characteristics were often known to the department when babies but were 'lost' on starting school only to be referred again later. As stimulation at the correct developmental stage (i.e. in the myelinisation process) is beneficial, this points up the importance of early identification of those children who are still having difficulties at school entry.

For this project, it was felt that a process oriented approach would be appropriate. Laszlo et al (1988) claimed to have found that it was possible to raise children's performance or motor tasks with as little as 1.5 to 3.0 hours training and the improved competence generalised to similar tasks. (The effect that was demonstrated could have been due to improved self esteem and was much more marked in the kinaesthetic than in the spatial or temporal areas). M's general lack of physical control would not easily lend itself to the detailed task analysis necessary for the behaviourist, task-oriented approach. Simpler skills such as putting on a coat had already been acquired. Some kind of non-specific improvement would be necessary for more complex skills such as handwriting.

The programme was operated for two 10−15 minute periods each day, morning and afternoon. Most of the work was done in the dining room, immediately outside the classroom door, but for three sessions each week advantage was taken of the stepping stones, hopscotch, shape and letter markings on the school playground. A large queue would form to participate, but it was ensured that the proposed experimental group got most practice. The group was taken by several 'helping Mums', and NNEB students and a learning support teacher who became interested, as well as by the teacher researcher.

Three children were selected from the results of the 'tramline' test to make up a group with M. It was important to segregate them during the programme in order to prevent them being demoralised by competition. These were D, J and C.

D, a solitary boy was usually found in the book corner or playing trains by himself in a remote part of the playground. His mother had expressed her concern that he 'didn't mix'. He was showing good ability at reading and number, but his writing was ill-formed. M later tried to befriend him, but it often ended with D running to the teacher in tears.

J, a girl who was constantly falling (whilst falls are commonplace in the early months of school as children adjust to the space in the playground and the numbers of other children, J was noticeably more accident-prone). Her mother took her to the doctor and she was diagnosed as knock-kneed and having a 'lazy' eye.

C, a very plump boy who appeared both mentally and physically slow. His concentration in stories and lessons was poor, but he was content to sit and stare about, without disrupting the class. His self-help skills were very poor. On one occasion, after P.E. he managed to get his trousers on inside out, shoes on the wrong feet, cardigan upside down and shirt missed out completely. He appeared to be very 'behind' in directional and motor sequencing development. He reacted to M's boisterous overtures quite aggressively.

Outcomes

The programme ran from Christmas to Easter with no breaks apart from half term and weekends – not easy to achieve with school functions and a crowded timetable.

Scores improved for all the group on all 'scorable' activities except for M's target throwing which remained very wild. Beanbags usually soared up to the ceiling! Rank order of the experimental group improved slightly on the two items on which they were re-tested against the whole class (tramline test and number of times children 'stepped off' wide balance bench – 'narrow balance bench' although this proved impossible to score as a steady hand had to be offered in case of accidents). There was a marked improvement in shoe-changing ability after two attempts, at least, every day. The worst performance by all the group, apart from J, was in the motor sequencing tasks. They frequently had to be prompted for the second element of the sequence, and remembering three was quite beyond them. Some of the rest of the class who joined in on the playground were capable of four or five with practice, particularly the girls.

Just as significantly, M's day to day competence showed signs of improvement. He developed the patience to complete the Montessori staircase, fill a whole pegboard and once actually won the 'dead dogs' game where the aim is to lie immobile while everyone else is eliminated for slight movement. He also received praise for his behaviour at prayers and lunchtime. (The school has a policy of constantly 'reinforcing the positive' and children are often sent to the head and other colleagues for praise for work or behaviour).

On the other hand, the teacher researcher's diary shows that the number of disruptive behaviours displayed by M remained resolutely at around three per day. An improvement would have been expected but an analysis of the type of incident reveals, if anything, an escalation in aggressive behaviour. He several times threw other children's gloves and scarves over the fence or on to the roof, and began to seek out A for confrontation and so to interrupt other children in the class.

Conclusions

The programme appeared to fail in its original intention − to improve M's behaviour. Perhaps the time scale was too short; perhaps the training should have been combined with a behaviour modification programme aimed at a specific area, perhaps a token reward system. On the other hand Laszlo et al (op cit) reported that a few children, after training, became not only more outgoing and confident but more self assertive and aggressive. Perhaps increased aiming skills improved the effectiveness of his attacks!

Simpson, however, pointed out that she had learned several useful 'wrinkles' − putting books on a non slip pad, anchoring paint pots etc with a blob of sticking putty, tilting books to the child's preferred side etc. Conscious thought had been given to the issues raised in the school, and colleagues had discussed the children in the light of their own experience. The children themselves certainly enjoyed the programme and sometimes asked to do their 'exercises' again.

The design of the study would have been improved by ranking the children and putting alternate children into control and experimental groups. It would have been difficult however to exclude one group from the programme in normal classroom conditions. Other factors and variables could have been identified with more clarity but it was felt that an attack on the behavioural symptoms would not have succeeded without some attempt to improve the cause of them – the physical problems. Simpson indicated finally that more knowledge about the way in which motor, spatial and temporal development underpin school progress would be of great use to the classroom teacher.

13. Medical Problems and Educational Achievement, with Special Reference to Diabetes

A. Spolton (1988)

Background

This teacher researcher decided that for her area of investigation she should observe a child in her class (C). She stated that C had been causing some concern since Spolton had taken over the class in September. Her reading was poor and she was struggling to cope with the books a comprehensive reading scheme provided. Although she had given her more books at the same level hoping to combat the problem, she seemed to work through the books rather quickly and showed no signs of improvement. Her written work was very weak, often making no sense and her spelling was inexplicable. She seemed interested only in the speed at which she did her work rather than the quality of the work which she produced. Taking the non-verbal test results from previous years as a general pointer, it was felt that C's performance in English fell short of what would be expected from a girl of average ability. The teacher researcher wondered if there was a connection between her approach to her work and the fact that she was a diabetic. Her decision to take part in the Action Research Network gave an opportunity to investigate that theory.

Action Research

The first task to diagnose the problem was to investigate the possibility of a connection between poor educational performance and ill-health in a child especially with regard to diabetes. Male and Thompson (1985) dispelled that theory immediately, stating 'There are no learning difficulties specifically associated with this condition.' They went on to list symptoms if a drop in the level of sugar in the blood was occurring, several of which could affect a child's learning if they persisted.

However, since C had a well regulated management of her insulin level it was obvious that although she was a diabetic, this was not the present cause of her problem.

Since it appeared that C's problems did not lie in her diabetes and her hearing and sight were normal, it was decided to investigate the problem from a purely educational point of view. She therefore decided to study her records and to talk to her parents about her work and general attitude to school.

The project began by investigating C's previous performance in English. These showed that she had made very little progress in her reading in the last three years and that her verbal and English scores had gone down, whilst her non-verbal scores had actually improved. Spelling scores stayed the same.

C's previous teachers were consulted. Their general opinion was that as an infant she seemed to have 'patchy' days. Sometimes she was lively and alert and on other days she was rather passive and uninterested. She seemed to find new ideas hard to cope with and her reading was based on guesswork or look and say rather than phonic understanding. Her attitude to work varied from periods of hard work to stubbornness and a lack of application. Hard work meant that she attacked the work and rushed to finish it without any regard to quality. The suggestion was that she was only interested in getting through the work without making any effort to ensure it was correct.

C's parents endorsed much of what the other teachers had said. During home reading times they had attempted to make her read more slowly. They had noticed that whilst C often enjoyed writing stories at home they were always completed quickly. In fact they seemed to feel that it was part of her attitude to life that things should and would be done quickly whether they be school work or tasks done at home.

From this research several points emerged. Firstly C's problems in English seemed to be long term. They had begun almost from her first entry into school and the problems she had in the class were mostly the same ones she had had in the infant classes. However, now she did not display stubbornness or lack of application to work. She seemed to want to improve her work but did not know how she could achieve this.

At this point it was decided to attempt to tackle the problems C was having with both her reading and her written work. To make such a project manageable it was felt wise to concentrate on one area. A decision was therefore made to begin with her reading and employ strategies to slow down her method of tackling reading. This was done by listening to her reading every day and both encouraging her to read slowly and also look carefully at all the words. Further, she was encouraged to take notice of punctuation marks. It was clear that this was not likely to work unless it was endorsed with strategies which ensured she did these things whenever she read.

It was arranged for C's parents to begin a programme of paired reading at home and good readers were recruited in the class to help C by running a paired reading situation in the classroom.

C was limited in the amount of reading she did at any one time so that she realised that rushing did not get her through the book more quickly. A prepared passage strategy was activated so that C could work on part of her book and when she was ready would bring it to be listened to. She knew that if she did well she would be awarded team merit marks and thus incentive rewards were introduced for slow, careful reading. A policy was adopted of reminding C each time she read of what points she was working on and this worked very well.

Spolton employed these strategies for a period of two months. She stated:

> Although C's reading improved in that she no longer rushed, she observed the punctuation marks and also looked more carefully at the whole word rather than the initial consonant, I felt that she lacked phonic knowledge and this was hampering her further progress. This led me to decide on another line of investigation and to help me I consulted the Remedial Teachers' Handbook. The chapter on assessment of reading skills dealing with children whose reading age was 8–9 suggested that a diagnostic test would give an analysis of reading error highlighting various areas which needed reinforcing. I therefore conducted a similar test.

This showed that C indulged in contextual guessing from initial sounds, had a glaring lack of phonic knowledge and substituted one sound for another.

Using this analysis as a pointer, it was followed up by giving C a phonic blend checklist to see where she showed specific weaknesses in her phonic knowledge. Using this further information, a remedial work programme was worked out using the workbooks and cards from the LEA reading service.

Strategies were also employed in the hope of encouraging C to tackle her written work in a slow and careful manner with a view to producing more thoughtful and accurate pieces of writing. This was done firstly by giving her time on the computer using the word processor to write her stories, letters and poems. (The idea behind this was to slow down her actual writing time hoping this would make her think more about the writing and spelling.)

Secondly, she was encouraged to place limits on writing – smaller amounts to encourage quality not quantity and also by asking her to write only a line and bring it for marking and checking.

Outcomes

Her work was analyzed from the computer printouts by classifying the mistakes and numbering them. There was no significant difference between work done on the computer and work done in her book. The largest number of errors were spelling mistakes. These included guessing with no obvious use of phonic knowledge, missed word endings and words with the same initial sound being used instead of the intended word. Other errors included lack of capital letters and grammatical errors but these were far fewer.

The second two strategies produced the best results. Limits on the amount of writing and writing line by line made C more careful about the work she produced. When her work was discussed, she responded immediately by trying to avoid mistakes or correcting them verbally as soon as they were identified. The introduction of a marking code enabling children to identify their own problems and correct them also made C aware of the mistakes she repeated in her written work.

Again these strategies were employed for two months and certain aspects of C's work began to improve. She worked more slowly and carefully and no longer omitted all the full stops and capital letters. However her spelling still gave cause for concern so C was tested for spelling weaknesses using McNally and Neil's 1st hundred words and 2nd hundred words list. The errors that were highlighted were made into a spelling programme and the methods C used to learn them followed the 'look, cover, write' method advocated by Cripps and Peters (1991).

Conclusions

The main emerging issues from work with C were that there are many children within a class who may not have been specifically identified as children with special needs but who may actually have a special need which must be identified and dealt with. Secondly, children in this category may often fall in the middle range and teachers must be aware of this and make special efforts to provide for these children. It is also important to point out that each problem needs special strategies designed specifically to help that child and these may change after investigation and analysis of the results.

An analysis of the dilemmas of working with C in this project was threefold. Firstly, in a large mixed second and third year class with its fair share of low achievers the teacher researcher had a limited time to devote to C. Because one of C's strategies in class was to work quietly and to keep her head down, the action plan for that day was sometimes overlooked. The arrival of several new children into the class, including a non-reader with all the obvious attendant problems, limited the amount of the time that could be allocated to C and because the amount of improvement shown was slight and had taken so long to emerge there was a tendency to become despondent about the pace of progress. This was compounded in part because the network support database did not give specific information about the children who rush through their work related to reading problems.

Developing Liaison Between Schools and Between School and Home

Close liaison between schools has a long history and the staff in all phases of education have for many years helped to settle pupils into their new schools. Strategies to encourage this process have included inviting staff from the new school to talk to pupils, taking pupils on visits to their new school, conducting lessons in their new school and talking to the liaison staff about their new entrants.

More recently the need for such liaison has been heightened by the impact of the National Curriculum, which has attempted to integrate the learning experiences of pupils in mainstream schools into a continuous process throughout the years of compulsory schooling.

Liaison, however, is not just about changing schools but also about the relationship between school and home. Parents are generally keenly interested in the success and progress of their child at school.

Liaison is an important feature at all stages of a pupil's experience and development. The projects discussed in this section illustrate this aspect throughout these stages. Tweddle (1990, 1991) in a two phase study highlighted the importance of liaison for the pre-school child and its parents, while Tune (1989) concentrated on the need for effective home school liaison in the primary school. Cooper and Vickers (1989) looked at the effects of transfer to secondary school of a pupil with special educational needs during his first six months there. Stakes (1990) investigated the changing perceptions of one pupil at the time of his transfer from primary to secondary education. Hollingworth (1991) pursued a similar theme when she questioned the new Year 7 intake at her school. She then undertook a follow-up study some four months afterwards to check on their feelings at that time.

14. Involving Parents and Children in the Pre-School Stage

H. Tweddle (1990, 1991)

Background

This teacher researcher was the special needs co-ordinator at her infant school. Following the work of other network members, particularly Tune (1989) who had concentrated on the need for effective home/school liaison in the primary school and Cooper and Vickers (1989) who looked at the effects of transfer to secondary school of pupils with special educational needs during the first six months there. In this research at the pre-school stage of education, she focused her attention on involving parents and children in a programme of induction.

Tweddle was concerned that many of her pupils began their school life with recognisably low attainment. In each reception class there was a small group who exhibited very introvert or very aggressive behaviour, who obviously needed much play and talk, and who were not ready to begin the simplest level of the school's schemes. They needed the opportunity to develop social skills, and to have a great deal of enriching experience in language and in concept building activities.

In order to 'remediate' the Special Needs problems during the year, parents, ancillaries, and other available adults had been invited to help groups with games or other activities. The greatest benefit appeared to come from the talking and attention the children received rather than necessarily which activities they participated in.

It seemed that no new kits or equipment were appropriate to supporting this situation. The important need was for the time consuming work of talking to and getting to know the children. She comments:

> I read about 'nurture' groups in the Warnock Report (1978) which had been started in a number of primary schools in London for children approaching or over the age of five who are socially and emotionally affected by severe deprivation in early childhood and decided to explore the concept further to see if there wasn't some way we could influence the level of attainment of our new starters. My idea was to set up a group for parents and children, concentrating on those with special difficulties, a nurture or opportunity group to compensate for their limited experience by offering advice, training and example.

This idea was endorsed by the Warnock Report which commences:

> The presence of wise and sympathetic parents and a favourable domestic setting will provide the best start in life. But if parental support is lacking or living conditions are unfavourable, compensatory measures may be needed if a child is to have the benefit of good care and education.

However, Tizard, Mortimore and Burchell (1980) argued:

> Children in deprived areas are often said to arrive at school barely able to speak, and lacking a knowledge of basic concepts. There is good reason to believe that this view is something of a myth.
>
> Further, they indicated that research by Francis (1975) and Bernstein (1971) amongst others supported the idea that most children have a sufficient grasp of language structures and usage to undertake the task of reading. Tweddle indicated that in her school it was a minority who had not developed these skills who made up the special needs cases. These were some 8 per cent of each year's intake. It however became apparent that to try to set up a compensatory group for specific cases would be inappropriate for the present. Firstly, there was no machinery to identify the children in need. Secondly, it might be seen as 'putting the parents right' where they had failed to bring up their children properly. Further, it would require much work in preparation of materials, and in training colleagues and the parents. It was also important not to lose opportunities to welcome the other parents and children.

Warnock (op cit) wrote of the experience of Parent Workshops:

> The leaders of the project . . . recognise however that, even under expert guidance, parents' workshops are not always successful. They must meet the needs of parents who will differ in background, personality, intelligence and ability to express themselves, and a high degree of skill and sensitivity is required to run a small group of this kind.

It was felt that the school was not ready for this kind of role yet. Further information from other sources on pre-school links was needed. Many of the documents received suggested ideas for setting up pre-school clubs open to all prospective starters, or describing other schools' experience of this work.

Tweddle described the current practice in the school. She stated:

> This involved having parents take part in a wide variety of activities, and encouraging all parents to join in, in whatever

capacity it suited them. If we were to extend to the pre-school children and parents, we had to maintain this broader policy. In our school we had no nursery provision, but we did have an Early Admissions class. Our annual intake was approximately 75 children. We had an induction programme during each summer term of two or three afternoon visits where the new intake pupils visit their classrooms and the parents go into the hall to talk to the Headteacher. They were all given a booklet describing the school routine and policies. Each of our two local playgroups made a half day visit with the incoming children, too. Warnock suggested ways we might alter our practice. They included home visiting, teaching services, parents' workshops, playgroups and opportunity groups, nursery schools and classes and day nurseries. While we cannot as a school provide these, we need to have good liaison with these facilities locally.

Bereiter and Engleman (1966) indicated that to support this approach several activities were necessary. These included home visiting, pre-school clubs, asking parents' help to write the school booklet, having a parents' notice board, making films or videos for and with the parents, having a library hour for parents, and having a toy library. As a consequence, the areas that it was felt needed evaluation were:

- The induction procedure for the new intake;
- liaison with the playgroups, the local support centre, the Welfare Officer, Social Services, Health workers, Doctors, etc;
- documentation, booklet, forms, letters, etc;
- general home/school liaison policies;
- attitudes towards the parents.

Such a comprehensive evaluation would certainly benefit the school in the long term, but it would be an enormous undertaking, and be quite unrealistic for this small scale action research project.

Very quickly I realised I had taken on rather too much. It was through discussion with colleagues at the next Action Research meeting and through my reading that alternative strategies were suggested. These included setting up a pre-school club, starting home visits, inviting our current parents in to ask their opinions about what they felt would have been a helpful induction, sending a questionnaire to get information from local schools about their intake policies, their approach to special needs from the pre-school stage, their school booklet, etc. and visiting local playgroups and asking for their cooperation.

After considering each of these strategies it was decided that the best move was to hold an investigative meeting with staff, with a view to testing opinion, seeking individual co-operation, and arousing awareness of these concerns. This again was consistent with approaches advocated in the Warnock Report:

> If ordinary nursery schools and classes are to make satisfactory provision for children with a variety of special needs, a number of conditions must be met. First the attitudes of the Staff and the parents of all the children must be favourable . . . The accommodation and equipment must be suitable. Thirdly, staffing ratios for non teaching as well as teaching staff must be generous. Fourthly, the implication for all children of accepting children with different disabilities and difficulties must be carefully thought out by all those concerned. Fifthly, teachers must have regular advice and information from specialist and advisory staff.

Action Research (Phase l): The Staff in the School.

Tweddle outlined the problems associated with meeting these conditions. She said:

> Bearing these factors in mind, and knowing that staffing, accommodation and equipment were already stretched to the extreme in our school, I felt sure that any proposals I might make to our staff could meet with some resistance. Therefore the first part of my planning was to write down the points I expected to be raised for and against increasing our pre-school liaison procedures.

She was not sure how to approach the staff meeting. She stated:

> I wanted to arouse in the staff a positive mood; I wished to have the notion of closer and earlier pre-school links become their own. I formulated a list of questions and points which I felt would lead to a common conclusion — that early and supportive relations with parents will foster better attitudes towards education, and promote a sharing interdependence of responsibility between us for the child.

Further she selected from the books she had read so far certain passages that she could refer to during the staff meeting.

She met with her Headteacher and they decided to choose the question, 'What factors do you consider affect your pupils' progress?' She expected that a positive attitude or practical help from the parents would be one of the responses.

I felt very cautious; I did not want to arouse a negative reaction. I needed to stress that this was just a tentative exercise as yet; that any outcome of this meeting would be a simple practical one, if any, and that further ideas, or spin-offs, resulting from this would provide us with long term plans. I hoped to recruit sympathetic members of staff to act as a steering committee for this work. As Inset Co-ordinator I had another channel at my disposal to achieve this aim quickly, and I was able to discover two willing and enthusiastic volunteers.

To encourage the interest of the staff in the school she arranged to visit the feeder playgroups and all the staff visited a local play-group. Finally she made out a draft questionnaire to send out to schools.

Outcomes

The staff meeting was held at a lunchtime for about three quarters of an hour. The discussion was based round the issues which related to the difficulties of pupils coming into school and making good progress. Responses from the staff indicated that the development of trusting relationships, their physical well-being and matching the tasks in school to their general potential were of importance. However there were no clear answers in connection with the plan which Tweddle had in mind for this project. She reflected on this:

Perhaps in hindsight it might have been better to ask that question on paper prior to the meeting so that I could then have arrived at the meeting prepared to talk about the way in which early parental involvement would be of benefit in each of these directions. Nevertheless, in the event I moved on to the research. I decided to state my case. I said I felt that a child was affected by family attitudes towards education and that these influenced their own attitudes and readiness for school.

Then 'taking the bull by the horns', she suggested that the image of the school, however approachable it may wish to be, was probably seen by parents as one of authority, with the weight of the 'system' behind it.

From this a lively discussion ensued, with all staff contributing, resulting in the unanimous conclusions that schools tread a fine line of diplomacy and that they do need to evaluate themselves and check that they are making efforts to be unthreatening, approachable, and to avoid being dogmatic.

This led on to discussing the school booklet. Staff talked about how much they had already improved relations with parents recently through the curriculum topic meetings, invitations to class assemblies and concerts, through involving parents in the classroom and with resource and construction work, and through a shared reading programme.

Discussions took place about intake procedures, the difficulty of large numbers, and how it already took several days to fit all the visits in. One colleague pointed out that, in her experience, it was the parents you most want to see who don't come. The issue of home visits was raised. Another colleague said other schools do this locally, but they have extra non-teaching staff to cover it. It was necessary for the Head and the co-ordinator to reassure the staff that they were not expecting them to undertake such work – not without careful planning and consideration, and not in the immediate future.

The benefits to be gained from, and the difficulties posed by, trying to improve parental involvement were also discussed. Concern was expressed that the school would get limited results, or none at all, in affecting parents' attitudes. However the Head said that other schools' experience had shown a long term improvement, over a period of about five years.

Some of the staff who had been parents themselves were particularly sympathetic to the notion that schools can be forbidding places. They said that they had had misconceptions about the best way of treating their own child at the pre-school stage, and that they would all have welcomed the chance to share ideas with other parents.

The Head suggested that in time the school could think even further, to offer an activity pack service, or a toy library, book sales, social events, and coffee mornings, with creche facilities and perhaps utilise the Community Centres for these developments.

In spite of the limitations of the situation, the staff were definitely positive about seeking closer relations and said they would be in favour of a sub-committee which would discuss possible strategies to facilitate this approach.

All the staff had made visits to the local Centre and had been most impressed by it. The teacher researcher had visited two playgroups and was enthusiastically received. They were both keen that close liaison be established. They spoke about the difficulties of getting parents to help; one playgroup found the parents were very willing, while the other found them most reluctant. They also felt the need for links with social and community workers, there being no facility for this as far as was known. This was an area to be investigated further. Concern was also expressed that children undergo a three-year-old screening which is outside both the home and playgroup situation, and the playgroup leaders felt that this probably led to rather doubtful results and performance. They would welcome the aptitude part of the test being carried out in the familiar surroundings of the playgroup and wondered if this would be feasible.

When she reported back to the staff on the visits, they too welcomed close liaison with the pre-school facilities as a priority and something that they could and should try to build into their normal procedure.

Conclusions

Tweddle evaluated this process in these terms:

> It was important for the staff to have the opportunity to join in an initial evaluation of our situation, and to discuss current findings and ideas on how to foster better home/school relations. I believe that it would have been a mistake to try to impose a new policy without consultation. The staff needs to be involved at the assessing and planning stage in order for them to be able to air their views. The notions of respect, worth and value are central to relations between the staff, the children and the parents. The framework and rigour of the action research network and process have enabled me to approach this project in a reasoned and organised way. It helped me to identify an appropriate starting point, and broadened my access to relevant literature.

Action Research (Phase 2)

Tweddle was able to continue with these developments during the next school year. She pointed out that having further discussed the findings of the first phase of this study with her staff colleagues, it was found that there were several avenues which might be explored to improve their practice. These were concerned with home visiting, organising parents' workshops or self-help groups, closer liaison with playgroups, holding parent and child play sessions and improving communication with families.

Some of these ideas lent themselves to their situation, whilst others were much too ambitious. The school felt confident in attempting certain ideas. For example, in addition to the playgroups visiting school with increased invitations to do so, visits were made to the playgroups to meet staff and children there. Secondly, the School Starters Booklet was altered by reducing the text and having a cartoon or picture on each page.

The major area which was tackled was item four of the original action plan: 'Holding Parent and Child Play Sessions'. In this way it was hoped to be able to influence the willingness of parents to play with and talk to their children. It might also help to improve parental involvement, affect parents' understanding of what staff were trying to do, give children an earlier and gentler chance to become accustomed to school and help the staff become aware early on of children with special abilities and difficulties that would need to be accommodated. However, it was also felt there were problems of space, staffing, resourcing and organisation to overcome.

By allocating a school INSET day, a visit was made to the local special needs unit. Whilst there, the research project was discussed with the head of the unit who gave encouragement to overcome the various difficulties in trying to hold the play sessions. Another local parent and toddler group offered a visit and gave much information on organisation and practical hints.

One fortunate consideration during this school year was that there was a spare classroom and this was felt to present an ideal situation 'to have a go':

> We had to decide on the number of sessions, the timing of them, the best way to staff them and a plan of activities possible and a list of resources, plus a reshuffle of the timetable with the cooperation of the staff. We needed to consult playgroups to ensure cooperation there. Also we needed to plan how to advertise the sessions with letters, posters and meetings.

Tweddle had the idea of basing the afternoon's play on a different topic each week so that the wall displays and activities offered would give a broad example of how learning takes place.

During the three weeks before half term, two local playgroups were contacted and arrangements were made to see the parents whose children were due to start in September. A list of expected names was supplied. These were split up into attendance days (their 'classes') deleting those they knew had places elsewhere and informing the school of those applying for other schools.

This procedure was successful:

> Each playgroup displayed a poster about the play sessions. The playgroup ladies couldn't have been more helpful, and it was because of them that the meetings were so successful. Each

playgroup had gathered together the relevant parents for me and had them sitting waiting. I tried to make my talk friendly and relaxed and I took along a list for parents to say which afternoons they wished to attend.

Twenty children were invited each day Monday to Thursday together with their parents, leaving Friday free. Very few were able to decide on the day immediately, but they rang school afterwards to request a day. Lots changed their minds too. Parents were asked to volunteer to come early on their chosen afternoon in order to help set up the sessions.

Letters which the playgroup distributed offered a place at school and asked for confirmation of take up, and a copy of the child's birth certificate. Further, it explained the purpose of the play afternoon sessions and asked for volunteer helpers. Parents or an adult must attend. Sessions were free, and there would be a different topic per week, plus a newsletter. It asked parents which afternoon they would prefer to come, or if they wished to ring up first, they would be given the daily and weekly programmes.

One playgroup was contacted by phone and provided the names of those attending who would be coming to the school. They sent letters to parents suggesting a day to attend the new scheme and requested they phoned to rearrange if it was inconvenient. (Several parents did so).

At school a meeting was held to explain to staff the intentions of the day. These were: firstly, talking plans through with reception staff, the headteacher and the ancillary staff. Secondly, it was agreed to provide weekly information to go home. This was to be a pictorial task sheet, based on work by Mutusiak (1988), which would help give an indication of children's ability. Thirdly, it was agreed to have refreshments available at minimum cost. The headteacher intended to send out a letter to all parents (just in case some didn't attend) to arrange the formal meeting. Here she could talk to the parents and give out the booklets, etc. This would be organised in four small groups rather than one large group as previously and wouldn't be quite so traumatic if parents and children were now familiar with school. Reception staff were asked to drop in to play afternoons during their afternoon break if possible. The furniture in the classroom was rearranged and the boards displayed to indicate how an Infants classroom is divided into bays or areas.

The headteacher had arranged that both ancillaries would be in the classroom at 1.30 p.m. to set up things and generally supervise. It was decided to put two kettles in a classroom next door so that drinks could be served in safety. Once it was known who was coming, and on which day, daily registers were printed with one copy to the office and one copy to the playroom.

Tweddle described how the sessions were undertaken:

> Each day I had a plan of the activities to be laid out, and a list of items required for each. I cut paper and prepared special resources, leaving regular things such as water, paint and glue to the ancillaries. We had intended to utilise volunteer helpers, but in practice, I worked in the lunch hour so as to be ready, and our ancillaries insisted on helping too. This was fortunate as the families began arriving from 1.45 p.m. They certainly wanted their full time. They always seemed eager.

Outcomes

The headteacher, wishing to ensure that there was adequate staffing, released that teacher and the two ancillaries for the beginning of the afternoon. In the event, with all the parents there were just too many adults. As a result, the atmosphere was rather strained at the start of the first week's sessions; the answer to this proved to be music. She put on a tape from the 'Playschool' programme and this broke the ice. Also whilst the training had led staff to direct their attention to the children, she quickly realised she was making a mistake here and that she needed to welcome the parents and foster their confidence instead. Once everyone started to relax, the quality of involvement was generally extremely good. The parents looked at the books and activities displayed. They chatted with one another. The children settled happily. The afternoons evolved into a routine which was easy to fit into the school day. Having no session on Friday meant that staff could strip down the displays in order to change the boards over the weekend to give the room a new theme. The teacher researcher prepared picture labels and explanations and materials each week ready to mount them before Monday morning, and it was all surprisingly efficient.

The afternoons did not all go off without a hitch; the first session was crowded and noisy with many younger siblings attending too. In fact the staff decided to label prospective pupils so as to be able to recognise them, using sticky labels.

The serving of drinks helped parents to get to know each other. However, attendance did drop over some weeks with unbearably hot weather every day. Several fathers came, and they played very closely with their child. One particular group of mothers voiced reasons for not coming with their child e.g. that when they went to playgroup the children expected their parents to stay too; or that the children resented their parents being there. Fortunately those particular parents did not stop attending.

Members of staff did drop in daily to meet parents and children. During one enforced absence, two colleagues were asked to run the sessions. They were very anxious about it, needing written instructions as to the procedure that had been established, but in the event both said how easy it had been and that they had enjoyed it.

Conclusions

Tweddle summarised the project as follows:

> To the child we hoped to offer:

> – A longer, slower opportunity to get used to coming to school.
> – A chance to be close to parents whilst in this new situation, meeting new people.
> – A way of discovering what school's about.
> – A 'taster' to help them be eager to come to school in September.

To the parents we hoped to offer the chance to:

> – Introduce their child to school gently.
> – Meet other parents to compare experiences.
> – Play with things they don't have at home.
> – Be in school and see some of the subjects being taught and how we learn by playing games and talking.

All the families attended at least two sessions, while 50 per cent attended every session. Many parents did look at the work displayed and asked about methods of work, schemes, etc. Children with special needs, such as physical disabilities, low attention threshold, and those needing emotional or behavioural support attended these sessions.

On entry in September, the staff found the children noticeably quicker to settle. Partings from parents were far less traumatic, the children seemed especially confident, and as a group they were very sociable. After conducting this project she indicated that she will seek the opinions of the playgroup leaders and the parents as to how they felt the play afternoons went from preparation to school entry, by letter, questionnaire and discussion. But already it seemed from observation of the children's attitude and performance that the sessions had been very successful and well worth the effort.

15. Parental Involvement in the Primary School

M. Tune (1988)

Background

This teacher researcher also looked at the issue of parental involvement in the hope that in her school she could encourage improvements. She explained:

> I am deputy headteacher at the school, and therefore the headteacher and I discussed the actual role of the manager as to relationships with parents to establish what we were actually doing. From that discussion it was decided we should actively encourage some kind of parent contact, either by a formal Friends of School Association or informal but regular links in order to raise money for school funds, provide occasions for parent/teacher contact and to explain policy, curriculum, organisation, etc.

It was also felt important to keep the parents informed of school events, needs and aspirations and to talk to parents about their children. It was felt that this would help by providing access to the school for interested and concerned parents on a regular basis. Further, there was a need to recognise that public relations is an important aspect of the teacher role and it should include being ready to listen to parents and to attempt to involve them in the day to day running of the school as ancillary helpers. Beyond these features it was felt that it would help home/school liaison by showing the parents of new children round the school and taking care to explain policies, by being around at arrival and home times to talk to parents, having some out-of-school involvement in the school community and by making home visits when necessary. It was also important that by being aware of the various support agencies for families, united we would be able to pass on the information to them when necessary.

Action Research

After these discussions Tune comments:

> The headteacher and I attended a day course dealing with parental involvement. This course clarified points which had arisen from earlier discussions, and also provided food for thought regarding action strategies for further development of relationships with parents . . . We brought our school brochure up to date ready for

the new intake and visits were arranged to the playgroups in the village for the reception teachers. Strategies were discussed whereby more parents could be more involved in their child's learning . . . All teachers recognise that parents may have a useful role to play in the life of a school — both in helping the school in a general way and by helping specific children in a particular way. Parental help is focused greatly on reading and, therefore, we decided to explore this avenue as one of our strategies.

We arranged for a Senior Lecturer from a local teacher training college to come and talk to the parents about reading. This meeting was arranged in liaison with the Friends of the School, and a glass of wine was to be served — thus making the event sound attractive! The event was successful. This involved various workshop ideas with parents and a discussion on the beginnings of reading.

Outcomes

At the same time as this initiative was being pursued, the problem of 'paired reading' was being tackled. Newson and Newson (op cit) found that up to 80 per cent of the parents sampled helped their children to read in some way or other 'mostly without knowledge or help' of the teachers in the school.

More recently interest and attention have been focused upon an approach to reading which requires the active involvement of the parent, or parent figure, in the reading practice of the child. This approach is called paired reading, and recent articles by Topping (op cit) have described this approach in more detail. The reading material should be selected by the child and reflect his/her interests, including both fiction and non-fiction material and time for reading is chosen to suit the child and parent. The close proximity which reading together requires fosters a time for closeness, which benefits both parent and child.

This technique has enjoyed considerable success with pupils from six to fourteen years. Reading gains have been achieved which are reported to have ranged from 1.5 times normal to 7 times normal on accuracy and 1 times 12 on comprehension. Armed with this information the staff were willing to try a similar project. The Head of the local learning support service agreed to come and speak to the parents to set the project in motion.

Conclusions

Tune concluded from her observations and discussions that this project had helped the parents of children in her school to:

> come to understand more about their children's approach to reading which the school was trying to teach and above all, that the parents could teach the teacher something about parental involvement. The reading together strengthens the relationship between parents and children. By activating this project we are to have a better parental involvement than before . . . I have found the task to be a useful, critical and constructive exercise. I feel the groundwork on discussion at the beginning was very essential to provide a way forward. As a result I have a greater understanding of the term 'paired reading'.

16. Transfer from Primary to Secondary School

J. Cooper and P. Vickers (1989)

Background

Cooper and Vickers both worked in a secondary school. In their action research project they decided to investigate how one child with known special educational needs (but not statemented) coped with the transition from Junior to Secondary School. The timetable dictated that only limited support was available for the child under investigation and this support was shared by both authors of this research.

J arrived from his feeder school with a reading age of 6.5 years and a history of significant behavioural problems. He was fifth in a family of eight children and had a sister in the third year of the school. His father had left his mother when J was one year old and he now had a stepfather. He was cared for by his grandmother during much of his early life and her home had low material standards. There is evidence of retarded development during this period. None of the children in the family were robust but they were clean, well dressed and attended school regularly, suffering only minor physical ailments. The feeder school was unsuccessful in obtaining any meaningful direct contact with the parents.

J was small in stature and reminiscent more of an eight year old than an eleven year old in level of maturity. Three secondary staff all commented on the fact that J immediately brought himself to their attention when they visited his feeder school where he had specific reading help from the learning support service. He had been withdrawn for two half-hour periods per week along with two other boys from another class. However, a prior arrangement on a one-to-one basis had been more successful. J became silly and less diligent in the presence of the other two boys. Only slow progress had been made. He expressed his dislike of reading and often pretended he had read a book when in fact he had not. He would talk continuously if allowed and had a good imagination but could become very uncooperative when required to write. He was beginning to make some progress with spelling.

Action Research

On arriving in secondary school, J was given a series of tests. Overall, his attainment results were equivalent to that of an average nine year old with the exception of reading and spelling where he had barely reached the age of an average seven year old.

It was decided that it was appropriate for J to be given one period per week of individual help in reading and 'Fuzz Buzz' was chosen as the most appropriate reading scheme. J had not met this scheme before and it proved to be an admirable choice. In the first six months he reached Book 12 and in addition to reading, J commented frequently on the illustrations, often foretelling what was going to happen and also being highly amused by various events in the stories. Whenever 'Windbag' was mentioned J guffawed and the stories in the series seemed to be pitched just right for him. J also received support using appropriate 'Trend' books in normal mixed ability English lessons from time to time.

In the mixed ability situation with the class teacher, J demanded attention and was disorganised. He tried to make out that he was less able than he really was and hid behind the problem by saying that he could not read. The same device was used by J in other subjects. Written work was difficult to obtain and could only be produced with help. J pestered other pupils, was cheeky on occasions and often wasted time. He followed stories mainly by listening and could answer comprehension questions only on a concrete level. One able pupil in his group had related well to J but any paired work usually resulted in the able pupil doing the writing and J drawing the picture!

In Textiles he produced a very positive response. He was quick to grasp the operational procedure on the sewing machine and came in five or six lunchtimes to complete quite a complicated piece of work which was displayed. He also worked on a second piece of work designing an apron and a pencil case. He was imaginative and wanted his work to be different from that of other pupils.

In personal and social development work taken by the form tutor, J struggled, particularly with written tasks, needing much more time than his peers. He was a 'loner' originally but made friends with a female group and his general social integration improved. The tolerance of the group towards him varied. He cried when upset and on occasions became very stubborn. It was very difficult to obtain homework from J despite very precise teacher explanation. On one occasion a letter from parents stated 'homework should not be set for him because J couldn't read.'

An analysis of two consecutive English lessons was made. In the first, J was 'in a mood' as a result of an incident during registration. He was one of several pupils in the class who had not done their homework. The homework was the copying up of some work already checked by the teacher and therefore within his capability. He was asked to complete the homework for the next day. J's mood subsided and he came willingly for his withdrawal reading lesson during which he was very cooperative. On returning to the mainstream class, J was asked to copy some instructions on the use of apostrophes. He had not got his folder or his exercise book. His pen, when he finally got it out, did not work. The teacher loaned him one. He then made a very creditable attempt at joined up writing and managed to complete copying the instructions from the board.

In the second lesson J failed again to bring in his homework. The teacher made it clear that she was very annoyed with him and that he would be expected to work very hard during the lesson to make up for it. This he did, completing an exercise on apostrophes without making one mistake.

The severity of the reading problem manifested itself first in Mathematics. J stated that he could not read the booklet (SMP 11–16) and thus could not do the work. This behaviour gave rise to doubts about his ability to sustain reasonable classroom behaviour.

It was not possible for the special needs department to give regular support in Mathematics to this pupil and yet it was apparent that some form of support was urgently needed. The decision was taken to tape the booklets. His reaction was to be observed; would the tapes help him to participate fully in the work of the class? Objections to the tapes were voiced mainly because of fears that other pupils would be distracted by them but the objections were dispelled when it was pointed out that headphones were to be used.

The SMP 11–16 booklets lend themselves to taping. Sentences are short, key words are accentuated, and there is not too much printing on each page. Liberal use is made of diagrams and drawings which either complement the task or are essential to it. Practical work is a major part of the course and thus the reading is reinforced by doing.

It was decided that taped lessons were to be used on a trial basis to judge their effectiveness. It was hoped that this would help J's reading development to be assessed, as well as leading to an increase in confidence. The member of staff would be freed from the task of reading to him. The integration of J into the class could be facilitated as well as his development of self reliance. It was hoped that possible discipline problems could be avoided if the source of frustration, the inability to read the work, was removed.

Outcomes

The cassette recorder was introduced to J as a special aid developed specially for him. This appeal to his vanity worked well for much of the time – only rarely did he refuse to use the tapes and this was often due to incidents outside the lesson. At the outset it was made clear to J that this was an aid, not a prop to be used all the year. He knew that eventually it would be phased out. He learned quickly to assemble the headphones and cassette recorder and so made rapid progress.

The other pupils accepted his use of the equipment well. It was pointed out to them that many pupils in the school would use the equipment at some stage in their school life for a variety of purposes. An offer was made to provide a taped copy of the multiplication table for those still unsure as an example of its more general use. Many class members quickly saw that it was to their advantage if the equipment prevented J from disrupting the lesson.

The booklets were taped in their entirety but the text was amended and expanded as necessary (more work could be done on this). Key words and polysyllabic words were stressed and a Languagemaster was used to help with this approach. The booklets were in three or four week modules and each module took about an hour to record. The taping was largely done at home.

Feedback at first was at an anecdotal level. J appeared to be coping with the work and had considerable mathematical ability. He settled down quickly and was soon making positive comments about his work in Mathematics. However his ability was not reflected in his assessment test results when he was left to cope without reading help. Subsequent assessment tests were either taped or the supervising teacher helped J with any textual difficulties. Although the long term aim would be to enable J to read and understand an assessment test independently, the main concern was to obtain a true assessment of his mathematical ability.

The results J obtained indicated a significantly higher mark when the assessment tests were read to him or recorded. Obviously there may well be other pupils who were obtaining assessment test results well below their true mathematical ability because of limited linguistic understanding and this was considered to be an area worthy of further investigation.

At the end of the Spring term, J said that he no longer needed the tapes. He felt confident enough to tackle the books by himself.

The equipment for this approach is available in the majority of schools and in many cases forms an integral part of English GCSE and field work in History and Geography. Tapes are available at very reasonable prices. The location of sockets or the lack of them can, however, be a problem.

It is important that staff wishing to use taped material are aware that some pupils may perceive its use as a form of labelling. But careful planning can result in its use for all levels of ability thus eradicating this problem. The usefulness of tapes is more limited when lessons are not standardised. SMP Mathematics is ideal for the taped approach because for the majority of the year only one class is using one module at a time It is therefore easy to economise on the number of tapes required. The more standardised nature of work for the National Curriculum may lend itself to increased taped support.

Whilst this part of the project concentrated on the use of taped material in Mathematics, some taped literature books and worksheets based on text were prepared and it was hoped to develop the resources in this area as time allowed and the demands of the National Curriculum became clearer.

Conclusions

The study was considered worthwhile from both a professional and personal standpoint although it was recognised that it had been rather more subjective than objective. It emphasised the need to tailor special needs provision to the requirements of the individual child and the view that each child is an individual. The study indicated that a child's lack of ability should not be a limiting factor in using the full gamut of educational technology available.

J has said that he was happier at the secondary school than he was at his junior school and although there were occasions when he exhibited undesirable behavioural tendencies, he did not cause major problems for his subject teachers. He responded well to individual help and it is arguable that the judicious mix of support offered assisted J's integration and transition.

17. The Effects of Transfer to Secondary School on One Primary Pupil

R. Stakes (1990)

Background

This teacher researcher (the editor of this section) looked at the effects of transfer on a primary school pupil. His concerns focused on uncovering the feelings of the boy to elicit perceptions about the transfer. He hoped that this project would help to aid the process of transfer of pupils to his school in later years.

Action Research

The project was undertaken by interviewing the pupil on three occasions, both before and after transfer.

The first occasion took place while he was in his last term in primary school but before he had been to the school on his pre-transfer visit or had been visited by any of the staff from his new school. This occasion was used to discuss with him his major fears and apprehensions and his hopes and aspirations.

The second interview was organised before the end of the summer term, in the final weeks in primary school, but after the preliminary visit to the secondary school had taken place. This occurred after he had been visited at his junior school by his new deputy head of first year. This occasion was used to discuss the visit to his new school and that of the new teacher and also to ascertain his feelings on transfer at this point.

A third interview was arranged during the early part of the Christmas Term in the new school year. This occasion was used to discuss the actual change from junior school to secondary school, how things had gone, what problems (if any) had occurred and how realistic his apprehensions and hopes had been.

It was felt that the most appropriate approach to the overall research strategy would be through a semi-structured open-ended approach on all these occasions, when he could generally determine the topics of conversation, but yet would allow questions about certain salient features. In this respect, an overall framework could be made but the structure of it would not be predetermined.

Further, to aid discussion a series of photographs was used. These photographs showed typical scenes in the life of his new school and it was hoped that this would not only stimulate discussion but perhaps also bring out other underlying issues.

The interviewee also had the opportunity to check on interpretation of what had been said during his interviews afterwards by reading the initial write-up after each one was conducted and to make corrections where necessary. In the event no corrections were felt to be necessary at any stage, as he felt his feelings had been conveyed well. He also had the chance to check the final script and to make similar corrections – again he made no changes to the original.

D was a boy of eleven years and five months when the first of these interviews took place. He was the only child of professional parents. He had a strongly supportive home background. His junior school described his English as 'good' while his Maths provided more difficulties although they stated, 'there had been a recent improvement in this area'. D was an articulate boy with a wide vocabulary and a good general awareness who had expressed an interest in becoming a writer when he left school.

Outcomes

The first interview took place before D had visited the secondary school for his half-day induction or before any staff from his new school had visited his primary school to hold discussions on this subject.

During the early exchanges in this meeting D was, quite naturally, apprehensive both in connection with the impending move and this interview. He explained that he had already visited his new school once. This was to attend a carol concert the previous Christmas. His impression of the school at that time was one of 'darkness' and 'drabness'. The occasion had left him with certain negative feelings about the move to secondary school.

After the initial exchanges and an explanation of how these interviews might be conducted, D indicated that he had four key concerns about the change of school These were:

– the level of difficulty of the work which he might have to do;

- the formality of his new school compared with his present one;
- finding his way around;
- bullying.

D indicated that he expected the level of work in the new school would be much higher than that which he had undertaken in his primary school. He did not know quite how he was going to cope with this. This was D's key worry at the time.

The question of homework was also mentioned. D indicated that he expected to get homework but clearly, at this stage, had not thought much about it. He suggested that he was not sure how he was going to organise himself to do what was required.

The question of homework was also shown to be an important feature in the minds of those pupils questioned by Hall (1986) and Manders (1987). Hall indicated that 13 per cent of those pupils she had interviewed felt this would be a problem, while Manders research showed that 31 per cent of his pupils felt this to be the case. Interestingly, 28 per cent of Hall's respondents indicated that they were looking forward to doing homework.

D also indicated that he was apprehensive about learning a foreign language although he was reluctant at this stage to say why this was so. However he was looking forward to being taught History by a specialist, to doing literature and to using the new library.

D felt that his secondary school was likely to be more 'formal' than his primary. He was wary about how relationships with staff would be conducted and he expected that the staff would be 'more distant' than those at his junior school. His main concern was with his person-to-person relationships rather than with the institutional level of rules and regulations which might occur. In this respect he felt there would be very little difference between the primary and the secondary school.

D was also concerned about the different styles of teaching which he felt he would encounter in the secondary school. He expected that the style of his new school would be 'rather stricter and more formal' than he had been used to. He again expressed the view that the teachers in the secondary school would 'set harder work' and 'expect it to be right' more often than their junior school counterparts.

The school to which D was to transfer was, as is usually the case, much larger than his primary school and like many other pupils he felt that this would be a problem and would lead to him getting lost. Hall (op cit) indicated that this feeling was present in 35 per cent of those pupils whom she interviewed. Manders (op cit) produced similar figures which indicated that this problem affected 42 per cent of pupils at this stage.

D felt that he would, at some point, be able to find his way around his new school but was sceptical to some degree as to how long this would take.

D was concerned about the possibility of being bullied by older pupils in his new school He was also aware that other pupils in his class at junior school were concerned about the amount of bullying they might have to face in their new school. Those pupils with older brothers and sisters had been told stories on this subject and these stories had been spread round the year group. The evidence collected by Hall (who taught in the junior school which D attended) indicated that fear of bullying was a prevalent worry among pupils approaching transfer to secondary education. Her research indicated that 75 per cent of those questioned were worried about this. In Manders' study only 32 per cent of those questioned indicated that they felt this would be a problem.

The Photographs

D was shown a series of photographs of his new school and asked to comment.

These comments fell basically into two categories, those about scenes which he felt were realistic, like one of a lesson change in a corridor and shots of some boys running through part of the school yard, and responses to those he felt were unrealistic. Examples here included shots of a pre-school party arranged by 5th year girls as part of their GCSE course and one of a fight scene which he felt had been 'manufactured' for these interviews. One photo caused considerable interest. This was of two members of staff. D felt that these were older pupils in the school. He felt the staff 'looked confident'. He was not sure just how this photograph affected his views on his new school. It was pointed out to D that the people were, in fact, staff who taught in the school and he had some difficulty in believing this.

Finally, D was asked what he felt he would miss most about his junior school. His response was that 'there would be little he missed except possibly the rapport which he had with some of the teachers'.

The Follow-Up Interview

The follow-up interview took place some weeks after the first interview and at a time when D had visited his new school and had had a visit from the deputy head of Year 7 to his primary school.

This interview was markedly different in content and to some extent in tone from the first one. D stated that the general impression he had gained from his visit had been 'positive'. He stated 'it was good', he had 'enjoyed it more than he expected'. He added that although he had stated that his general impressions were these, and that they were different from his expectations, he 'really had no idea what his expectations had been!'

D was strongly affected by his feelings about those teachers he had met on his visit. He felt that many of them were 'putting on a show' for the benefit of the junior school pupils. They were 'acting hard' and some he felt were 'posing'. D also discriminated through the comments he made about the characteristics of those staff he had met. Of one he said 'she was nicer than (she) really is until someone was not paying attention'. At this point 'a different person emerged'. Of another he said, 'the person was not acting but fitted more into an image which was closer to my expectations'.

D also met one of the teachers who appeared in the photos he had seen. Here he drew a comparison between the 'apparent light-heartedness of the picture and the reality where he wanted to show a different image'. D felt that this image was more in keeping with his overall expectations of what the teachers would be like in his new school.

D added that some of his friends had been left with the same impression about those teachers they had met, 'they wanted to put on an act'. D also stated that he 'was not sure what impression he was left with'.

D clearly relaxed during the visit to his new school. He described his initial feelings on the day it occurred as 'being terrified'. During the talk (which started the visit) he described himself as 'still scared'. As the visit progressed and he went round the building he felt 'the place was getting friendlier'. He was, however, unable to explain why.

Of the tour round the school, D said that he was surprised at the number of pupils who were moving about as part of their daily routine, the number of classrooms and that there was not just one room for first years to work in (Maths, English) but that rather the rooms were used by all year groups.

D was questioned about his transfer in September in the light of his experience. He stated that he was 'not as apprehensive as he had been'. He explained that this was for two main reasons. Firstly, the tour had helped to allay his fears 'to some extent' and secondly, he had met pupils around the school who he 'recognised and looked settled in'. He described them as 'looking happyish'. He also added that bullying now no longer worried him as much as it had done previously. This may help to account for his feeling of the more friendly atmosphere he mentions above but no real connection could be made at this stage.

D was asked about his favourite subjects. He said these remained as before, at the time of the previous interview but that after the visit to the school he was looking forward to doing Home Economics.

The Third Interview

The third interview took place after D had transferred to his new school in the early part of the Autumn Term. This interview consisted of two main features:

(a) a discussion of the issues which D had found to be important during the first two interviews and which he could now comment on;

(b) features which D had found to be important, interesting or different about his new school.

D stated that the level of difficulty of the work with which he had been presented had been 'generally what he had expected'. It some cases the work was at a straightforward level while in other subjects it was much more difficult. Further, he explained, the level of difficulty did not always relate to whether he had undertaken this subject previously. He also felt that in certain subject areas a conscious effort had been made to simplify the work in order to settle the new pupils into a pattern of working and also to give them confidence.

D again expressed the view that his experience had been 'generally what he had expected'. He had found the formalities of the assemblies and the general expectations of the staff about movement and conduct around the school to be more difficult than in his previous school.

His most important concern, however, was over the varying teaching styles and teacher expectations he had met in his time-tabled lessons. He suggested that there was little conformity within the school in this respect and that the situation was far more diverse than previously. Different teachers set different demands and had different expectations, a feature which he described as being 'quite hard to come to terms with . . . I cannot believe they are all so different'.

Apart from the difficulties outlined above, D mentioned two other difficulties which he had encountered. The first related to finding his way around school. He knew (as indicated in previous interviews) that he was likely to find this a problem and initially this was the case. However, by the end of his fourth day in the school he felt he had 'got where most of his lessons were sorted out' in his mind. He felt this was about average for the year group.

The other difficulty related to false information and room changes from those indicated on the timetable. The class group in which he had been placed had to deal with this issue during the first two or three days in their new school and this had caused some confusion and anxiety to both himself and others in the group.

D stated that there had been considerable misinformation on bullying during the latter part of his time at junior school. He felt that often this had been deliberately spread by older brothers, sisters and friends of the new first years. He had encountered no bullying (either personal or among others) since his transfer to secondary school.

The other issues which D raised in connection with (b) above were that he missed nothing about his junior school and that he was enjoying some of his subjects, both those which he had previously experienced and those which were new. Of those which he did not like, one was an old one (History) and one a new one. He was not happy about History, despite having been looking forward to it, because he had already covered the subject matter in the junior school. D also felt that the role of the secondary school was very different from that of the primary school. He suggested that the staff in his new school were 'more interested in his overall character development' and they 'provided a different focus' from his previous experience.

He expressed surprise at the standard of behaviour met by other pupils in his new school both in lessons and outside them. They were better than he expected them to be. These included the behaviour of pupils whom he had known in his primary school.

He felt that the school dinners were better than in his junior school and he was surprised by their low cost. Dinner time did, however, provide some points of criticism. He did not like the sitting system, being last on the rota was difficult as he was very hungry. He also found the end of the lunch break both 'cold and boring'. He said, 'there is nothing to do'. The playground with its huts and wire mesh surrounds, he described as being like a 'P.O.W. camp'.

D indicated that he had made more friends since his transfer from junior school and that the library facilities (which he had been looking forward to) were also better. Overall his new school was 'entirely better than junior school' and generally the staff (particularly the head teacher) were 'human, helpful and friendly'.

Conclusions

It was clear from the series of interviews that D's feelings about the transfer from primary school were similar to those of many other pupils from larger cohorts interviewed by Hall (op cit) and Manders (op cit) and those described in work done by Gorwood (1985), Youngman (1986), Camsey (1985) and Smith (1985).

This series of interviews also drew attention to the point that during the six month period in question the thoughts, concerns and worries of those transferring from primary to secondary school do not remain static. Rather, these change as the information and knowledge about the new school develop.

All four of the major problems as foreseen by D in the initial interview had been reduced by the time of transfer and had disappeared to insignificance shortly afterwards. His initial fears and apprehensions were those of the unknown and were largely based on personal anxieties, misinformation, distortions and ignorance. Like the vast majority of his peers, he was able to take on and adapt to his new surroundings and the challenges which they presented.

D saw his move to secondary school as an important stage in his personal development and one involving essential differences from the experiences of his primary school. Yet despite this, the change also contained an essential continuity of experience in the process of his schooling. D had perceived secondary school in the first instance as a platform for change, in what he would be taught, how this would be done and also the different expectations that would be placed on him.

In practice this was, in some respects, true. New subjects, different teaching styles, varied teacher expectation and his perceptions of the changed role of the school all occurred. Yet in other circumstances he found the work, in the early weeks in his new school, to be similar to the level he had encountered in his primary school.

After his initial pre-transfer trepidation about the move from primary school, D's overall comments about his new experiences were positive. He was enjoying his new school. He had made new friends, enjoyed most of his lessons and found getting round the buildings much easier than he had expected.

However, it must be pointed out that these comments came shortly after the initial transfer and cannot be taken as a sign of continuing good feelings. The new school experience will undoubtedly produce its own concerns and difficulties for D. This would provide an interesting source of information which could form the basis of a follow-up study.

18. Transfer from Primary to Secondary School

P. Hollingworth (1991)

Background

In a similar project to those outlined by Cooper and Vickers (op cit) and Stakes (above), Hollingworth undertook a survey by questionnaire of pupils entering their new secondary school. Her decision was based on the research outlined earlier which indicates that most pupils have very real fears about the transfer from what has sometimes been referred to as the comfortable homely, secure environment of primary education to the 'brash impersonal, more cosmopolitan environment of secondary education'.

This action research project was used to investigate more fully the issues involved in transfer which affect the pupils and in so doing to see if there is room for improvement in this school's induction programme.

As special needs co-ordinator Hollingworth visited the three main feeder schools and made contact with or visited the others. In any one year the induction team may be dealing with up to fifteen primary schools. As part of that team she visited the three catchment area primaries. In addition, she contacted the Heads of all other primary schools sending pupils to them, and visited these when it was deemed necessary.

Action Research

Copies of the proposed questionnaire were taken to the three main feeder schools and permission was asked to administer it. At two schools she was allowed to do this herself and was able to introduce it, giving ideas and/or information both before and during its completion. The third school, which was the largest, asked for her to leave the questionnaires and the class teachers administered it. This may have had some influence on the results.

The questionnaire used was kept as simple as possible. There were questions on how they felt about the transfer, points which were of concern to them, what the junior school teacher could do to help, and what they knew of any help they may have been offered in helping with their transfer to secondary school.

Outcomes

An analysis of the data indicated a wide variety of answers to the questions and this led to difficulties in categorising the results.

In all, ninety-six children responded to the questionnaire, fifty-five from one feeder school, twenty-seven from another and fourteen from the smallest. They indicated that they would be transferring to two out of six local schools although the vast majority (88.5 per cent) were transferring to the school where Hollingworth taught.

Responses as to what these pupils were most looking forward to in their new school showed that meeting new pupils was the most important (58 per cent) and some 47 per cent were looking forward to meeting new teachers. But by far the most important feature, as indicated by other surveys on this topic, was participating in new subjects. Some 99 per cent of those questioned in the survey indicated this.

Other features which were mentioned included a choice of menu at lunch time (64 per cent), joining new clubs at school (18 per cent), school trips (15 per cent), and changing classes and teachers for different subjects (13 per cent).

Aspects of life in their new school which they felt the greatest anxiety about also confirmed other studies. Homework was a concern to some 67 per cent of those questioned, bullying to 58 per cent, and getting lost to some 40 per cent. Other problems included doing new subjects (36 per cent) – even though the vast majority had stated they were looking forward to this aspect in an earlier questionnaire – detentions (some 23 per cent mentioned this) and 14 per cent were anxious about meeting their new teachers.

This information bears out much of that already collected in this field. The 'new' school transfer is shrouded in horror stories and rumours of bullying. Measor and Woods stated 'the most notable feature of pupils' attitudes ... was one of anxiety. Expressions of being 'frightened', 'worried', 'scared' and 'nervous' about going to the new school were frequent. They believe that pupils see their whole identities at risk in the coming transition. 'Pupils feared loss of self and more distant treatment from teachers in the new huge organisation. Harder forms of work threatened their self-image as a competent person ... There is real fear of not coping at all, that it would be 'too hard for me' and homework threatens to encroach on pupils' private space and time.

Pupils were also asked in what way their teachers could best help them change schools. This question provided many ideas. Apart from those who did not know (26 per cent) or those who wanted no help, there was only one answer with a substantial score. Some 21 per cent suggested staff should be kind, especially on the first day. In future years Hollingworth suggests that it may be useful to take these answers a stage further by throwing them open to discussion groups, and trying to get some consensus of opinion.

The responses to the question relating to their knowledge of what was being done to ease their transfer indicated that the majority (54 per cent) had no idea at all. Some 34 per cent knew of the half-day visit which had been arranged for them, whilst 11 per cent knew that during their first year the school would try to put friends together to help the transition. Hollingworth, however, indicates that there may be some bias in the responses to this question as she visited one feeder school (the smallest).

The responses to the question 'Do you know what is being done to help you change schools without too much worry?' indicated that some 54 per cent of children interviewed at this stage didn't know what was being done. For those who had some ideas, 34 per cent indicated they were to have a half day in the school, 11 per cent that the teachers will try and put them with friends, 4 per cent that they would have lunch there, and 3 per cent knew of a parents evening.

Hollingworth pointed out that they had received very little information. The results, she suggests, were rather disturbing in that within seven weeks of leaving their primary school so many had little idea of what would be done to assist them. There is a thin line between starting too soon, getting pupils too excited and out of control when some weeks are yet to be employed usefully at primaries, and between leaving pupils 'in the dark' so that they become overanxious. She suggested that there was a greater need for Year 6 class teachers to be more involved in giving out information, especially of an Induction Programme.

Similarly to Stakes (op cit), Hollingworth decided to undertake one follow-up study and two weeks into the second term at the secondary school she gave a second questionnaire to all Year 7 pupils. This was not exactly the same group as the first for all Year 7 pupils were given the opportunity to complete a questionnaire whether or not they had come from the three main feeder schools. There were further difficulties because the school was experiencing a 'flu' bug which decimated classes. Also, the replies of one tutor group were misplaced. As a result of these problems only 61 per cent of Year 7 was included in the results.

For administrative reasons each form group was seen separately, using the form period time at the beginning of the day. Hollingworth explained the questionnaire to each group and the pupils began to fill them in, but most did not complete them. The form tutors agreed to give them more time and returned the completed forms to her at the end of a five day period.

The questionnaire was made up of the questions relative to the feelings and experiences after their transfer. Instead of leaving certain questions open-ended as on the first questionnaire, it was decided to give a few written suggestions instead of oral suggestions only. This was to ensure that the less able could be helped to answer without too much difficulty. This is an issue which will be discussed further later.

A question was asked relating to differences that pupils had found in their new school and what had most stimulated them. Examples of aspects of this for them to consider were provided. They included: moving around, new subjects, having different teachers and making new friends.

The responses indicated that fifty-six children (77 per cent) found having different subjects interesting whilst sixty-five (89 per cent) mentioned making new friends. Other aspects given a regular mention included having different teachers (68 per cent), moving around school (58 per cent) and choosing their own dinner (34 per cent). Some 10 per cent of the intake mentioned new clubs and trips out, while 7 per cent mentioned playing sport.

Four of the first had been given as examples. With hindsight Hollingworth would not write down the examples again. By so doing the subsequent answers may have been influenced and consequently the results biased. However, these results show consistency with those of others who have done work in this field.

In relation to the difficulties which the pupils had found, moving round school was the most significant feature; some 75 per cent of those questioned mentioned this whilst 56 per cent found following the timetable a problem and some 30 per cent had found meeting their new teachers difficult. Some 22 per cent mentioned difficulties with homework.

The school where the follow-up survey took place is split site and it was interesting that many pupils complained not just of moving around but specifically mentioned the trek across the fields to the Upper School. Although the timetables take account of this, it is difficult to see what the answer could be because many of the newer facilities in the arts and crafts were built on the Upper School site. To eliminate this movement, the pupils would be deprived of these facilities.

The pupils provided a number of ideas as to what new first years should be told before arriving at a new school. This was an open-ended question and the pupils were provided with certain ideas verbally which, it was felt, would help them.

The issues mentioned were knowledge about finding the way around the school (some 42 per cent felt this would be useful). 30 per cent mentioned that prior knowledge of their timetabled lessons and their homework timetable would have been useful. 27 per cent mentioned other organisational issues such as school clubs, house arrangements and uniform. A similar number would have liked to know more about the staff, while 10 per cent mentioned greater knowledge of the arrangements for school dinners.

The new intake were asked how they felt now about their new school and how, if at all, their feelings had changed since their transfer there. Hollingworth stated that this was a question which the pupils found difficult to answer. Sixteen of the seventy pupils (22 per cent) made no comment to this question, while of the remaining children some 44 per cent felt that is was fine once they had got used to the place and felt their way around.

Finally, a question was asked about any desire to return to primary school. The results indicated that 73 per cent did not want to return to their old school, some 8 per cent would have liked to, while 9 per cent made no response.

Conclusions

These results indicated that generally the pupils surveyed were positive in their views of the transfer in relation to their new subjects, being able to choose meals, meeting new friends and having new teachers. These are factors that need accentuating in the induction programme. However, for certain pupils, their views on transfer were negative in relation to homework, bullying, getting lost, new subjects and possibly being put in detention.

Obviously, these are areas of concern which need addressing, particularly when the head of year designate visits primaries. They are fears common to all and as other research has indicated, are not peculiar to this school.

The lack of knowledge the pupils showed regarding the induction programme was a problem which needed addressing. Perhaps the primary teachers could become more involved in the future. Instead of seeing it as an interruption to their normal working, it could be used more positively, more in-depth as a theme to be worked on during the last term of Year 6. This would encourage the teachers of Year 6 to become more actively involved in the induction process. At the moment the initiative rests with the secondary school, and the primaries seem to be passive recipients of what is offered.

When the transfer was complete and the pupils well settled, it was interesting to know what, on reflection, they found most exciting. These positive points need emphasising when discussing transfer with Year 6 pupils.

Other ideas which might be considered to ease the transfer of pupils include letters written by Year 7 pupils stating what they think about their secondary school to those in Year 6, especially in a rural catchment area; a link-up of Year 7 pupils with those in Year 6, so that each Year 6 pupil has someone, preferably from their own village, whom they could talk to and to whom they could turn especially during the first week at secondary school.

Although Year 6 pupils come to the school for half a day, perhaps this is not enough. From the pupils' responses to the second questionnaire it is apparent that they would have preferred a longer period at the school with the opportunity to follow a timetable and to participate in lessons.

A school in Dudley implemented a scheme whereby Year 6 pupils from all feeder schools were placed into two groups, visited the secondary school every fortnight, and were timetabled to use the secondary school's facilities. This happened on Friday mornings throughout the year beginning the second Friday of the Autumn Term. It may not be possible to do the same, but perhaps more thought could be given to a similar scheme in the Summer Term.

Further ideas which might be considered include someone to take new pupils round on the first day; the names of all the teachers and who teaches what subject (this is information which could be made available to the pupils as part of the Induction package); having available the menu for lunch on the first day – this could be given to pupils during the 'settling in' form period which takes place on the first day and pupils could then work out what they wanted or what they could afford, and the preparation of a video of the school which may have the advantage of showing pupils the layout of the buildings, the length of the walk between sites, and the facilities on offer.

Other ideas from those who have undertaken work in this area include primary teachers being more involved with the induction programme. For example, Nash (1973) found that the children's ideas of what secondary schools were like, prior to entry, were largely misconceived because teachers in primary schools shared these false impressions and passed them on.

Many education authorities rely on individual schools making their own contacts with their feeders. They do not issue any guidelines, or include advisers in the role of linking groups of schools and promoting continuity in the curriculum.

The ILEA (1985) suggested:

> Opportunities for the interchange of pupils and children should occur throughout the year, but should be intensified during the last few weeks of the Summer Term so that transfer is virtually complete by the end of that period.

From an article by Camsey (1985) the following problems and possible solutions included: moving around for lessons, following a timetable and knowing terms like 'period' and 'break'. The possible solutions included Year 6 pupils being given a record book in which to copy a timetable. In the Summer Term they 'move around' the classrooms for lessons.

Concerning homework, the solutions included Year 6 pupils being given practice in copying down assignments and a limited amount of homework being introduced in primary school.

Large numbers of subjects can be overwhelming. The possible solution here would be to introduce specialisation in Year 6, a feature already being made more likely by the introduction of the National Curriculum.

Difficulties over formal lessons were indicated and a solution here included practice sitting in one place, listening and making notes in Year 6, all looking for a more formal structure to the primary school day.

However, as the study by Measor and Woods (1984) points out, by the beginning of the second term, most pupils had successfully adapted to the new school:

> . . . in making their adaptations, pupils are learning one of the most important lessons in life − how to adjust to society, with all its inequalities, inconsistencies, irrelevancies − and how to make the best out of one's own interests. Too much direction and succour might subvert this lesson. In any kind of school there will always be things pupils have to learn for themselves.

Learning Difficulties

By far the largest number of colleagues who were involved in the action research networks selected a learning difficulty of an individual or a small group of pupils in their class as the focus of their work. The themes chosen were diverse, covering many difficulties exhibited by children. There was also considerable variety in the age range of the pupils that were the subjects of these projects.

The investigations have varied from attempting to alleviate speech difficulties with a child in the nursery school (Rowlett, 1988), to the problems of working on GCSE English texts with a pupils in a mixed ability class in a secondary school (Starnes, 1989). Other topics chosen included the development of reading skills (Turner (1990), Hall (1990), and Holland (1991)).

Stothard (1990) looked at the problems of a first year junior school child with spelling difficulties. Williams (1989) investigated the issue of teaching infant school pupils joined up hand writing, while Baber (1989) investigated the use of active learning techniques as a method of developing social skills in children with moderate learning difficulties. Kent (1988) looked at ways of developing colour matching in an infant age child in a special school, while Riley (1991) worked with the same age group developing strategies which she could use to teach rhythm to aid auditory memory for pupils with special educational needs.

19. Pre-Language Work: An Introduction

S. Rowlett (1988)

Background

This network member took as her subject a Nursery child, four years old, who had virtually no speech. The boy (C) had attended Nursery for approximately two terms; one term part time and one term full time. The full time place was provided at the request of Social Services. The school was provided with considerable information about his home background and upbringing. Rowlett described the pupil in these terms:

> When C. arrived at the Nursery he had very little understanding of language, very poor gross motor skills, had not been toilet trained, and did not know how to play with toys or other children.

He was a poor attender when he only had a part time place. Progress was very slow. Once he had been given a full time place his attendance improved. He began to show an understanding of simple language but still did not use it himself. His gross motor skills improved and his social behaviour was becoming more acceptable. The staff felt that he had now reached a stage where his speech should be developing, and it was felt that a specific programme of work was needed for him. C had been assessed by a speech therapist but was, at the moment, on the waiting list.

In order to help C, information was sought from the Derbyshire Language Manual and the use of both the Living Language Programme and the First Words Language Programme, (Gillham 1979).

The Derbyshire Language Manual is worked on a one-to-one basis. It begins at a single word level and introduces the child to common, everyday objects, beginning with the actual object. It then progresses to simple verbs, body parts, pictures of everyday objects and actions depicted in pictures. Activities are suggested for each area.

Living Language is a remedial programme for teaching spoken language. It contains three language teaching programmes – Pre-language, Starter Programme and The Main Programme. The pre-language children are those with virtually no use or understanding of language. The Starter Programme is intended for those children with a small vocabulary of single words and the Main Programme is for those children who are beginning to combine single words to form simple sentences. The materials provide both programmes of work and methods for monitoring progress. It suggests that the programmes be worked with small groups of children. Both Living Language and the Derbyshire Language Manual provide similar lists of the most common nouns and verbs used by young children.

The First Words Language Programme is very similar to Living Language and the Derbyshire Language Manual. It provides a list of the first words children learn and it suggests three teaching levels. These are related to demonstrating (focusing the child on the word and what it refers to), choosing language – the child shows an understanding of the word by making a choice e.g. choose one picture from three, and to using language – bringing the word into a conversation or improvised story involving dolls, models, puppets etc.

The programme sets goal words which are basically four words to be taught at one time but it was important to bear in mind that what can look like language comprehension in a child is often more a matter of understanding non-verbal cues e.g. facial expression, hand movement, tone of voice. Care must be taken not to 'give the game away'.

The main problem can be to motivate the child to talk. Often the actual objects and pictures used and style of teaching are motivation enough. If not, a variety of motivators may be used. These include: a puppet talking to the child or for the child to talk through a posting box where the object disappears and suddenly reappears, a talking teddy (which uses a tape recorder to immediately play back the child's utterances), and 'an apple and a worm' – the worm slowly appears out of an apple as the child makes a sound – and a home made toy e.g. a face with eyes which light up whenever the child says a word.

Action Research

After discussions with all the Nursery staff it was felt that C was showing signs that he had reached the stage in his development when words could be taught. A simple check list, similar to the Pre-Language Booklet of Living Language, was devised and this also suggested that he had the basic skills needed for language to develop.

The programme of work was to introduce four words at one time. The first set of four words were all nouns but the following sets would include one verb. The words were chosen from the Living Language Starter Programme and were words which would hopefully stimulate C.

Each session of work was to last for approximately five minutes. Obviously, this would depend on C's attention span. Two sessions per day was the aim whenever possible. Activities were designed for each set of goal words. These were based on the following strategy:

- Each object was introduced into a play situation and if necessary the function of the object was to be taught.
- Putting the objects away – (checking for comprehension e.g. 'Put the teddy away'; 'Find me the spoon').
- Pairs of objects ('Here's a teddy'. 'Where's another teddy?').
- Reinforcement of the activities outlined above (but using pictures of the objects or an object and a picture as a pair).

Finally, very simple stories about each word were used. Sometimes a puppet was used to help tell the story. These activities were carried out on a one-to-one basis. Sometimes this was a withdrawal situation and at other times the work was carried out in the classroom situation with other children observing and participating.

When all the activities had been carried out, C's progress was checked. A collection of unfamiliar materials was used including pictures taken from magazines, and line drawings of the goal words. The words were checked for use and understanding, and the data recorded on the check list. When this word became part of C's own vocabulary and could be heard in regular use in normal Nursery situations, this was also recorded on a check list.

Less formal but equally structured work continued alongside this programme. A list of C's words was placed in the staffroom so that all the Nursery staff knew the goal words. These words were reinforced whenever the opportunity arose in the classroom situation. The staff also added any comments to the list and any new words spoken by C.

As C is a small boy, the rest of the Nursery children tended to 'mother' him and give in to him if he squealed for a toy. A more positive approach to C was therefore encouraged from other children. For example, they were encouraged not to accept a squeal from him but to wait until he said 'please' before giving him a toy. They were encouraged to include him in their play as an equal and not as a baby or toddler.

Scrap books containing pictures of C's words were placed in the book area and the children were encouraged to look at these with C. and talk about pictures.

Outcomes

In the notes of a daily diary, Rowlett indicated that C concentrated well for ten sessions and was only restless during three. She comments:

> It did not seem to make any difference to him whether he carried out the work in the morning or afternoon. It was observed that the

day of the week had no affect on him. Often young children are tired by the end of the day and the end of a week and their concentration may be low. This was not true with C.

The evidence she collected showed that the length of time C concentrated gradually increased as he worked through the programme. C only attended school eleven days during the action research cycle. The total number of days he could have attended was twenty nine days. These absences did not seem to affect C's performance. After each absence he worked well and remembered all his words. This could be an indication that he had a good memory.

The programme appeared to have been effective. C was motivated by the objects and pictures themselves and did not need an external motivator. He enjoyed individual attention particularly looking at the pictures and scrapbooks, and was willing to say the names of the objects and joined in the 'conversation' whenever he wanted.

The lesson was usually lead by C and his favourite objects were always found first. He was never pressurized into learning situations. However, the chosen activity was always introduced unless he was particularly restless.

He learnt the first four words well. The next four words posed problems of differentiating between two of the words. More work was obviously needed in this area.

The rest of the staff found it useful having specific words to teach to C rather than a more general approach. For example, at dinner time his spoon was pointed out to him rather than all his cutlery. This way he was receiving constant reinforcement of the same words.

One of the most exciting aspects of this work was that C began to ask all the members of staff 'What is it?' at every available opportunity. He also learned to be taken to the toilet. This may appear to be a triviality but it was in fact a great help.

The older Nursery children became keen to help even if they did sometimes receive a bite from C. They held his hand in the playground, helped him climb apparatus and tried to make him talk to them. C began to imitate the noises they made during play. They were particularly keen to 'read' books to him and he was willing to participate in this 'game'.

It was hoped that the programme adopted in this action research project would improve all aspects of C's development and behaviour.

Conclusions

The main problem encountered was the number of absences of the child being investigated. The actual time available for the research was approximately thirty days but from that only eleven days were available to work with the child. Consequently it was difficult to draw any firm conclusions from the data available.

At the end of the project there were no motivation problems but if the research had been carried out over a longer period of time, these problems may have occurred and would have needed to be watched.

C progressed well on the programme of work but he may reach a plateau or his rate of progress may slow down in the future. If this is the case, a number of alternatives would be available. These would include: introducing only one or two new goal words at a time and working with a small group of children rather than on a one-to-one basis (this group may be children who also need a little extra reinforcement or a group of children who are confident in their use of language); involving another member of staff, enabling them to take over the programme of work, although here the problem may be in forming the relationship. Finally it may be useful to introduce a motivator e.g. 'talking teddy' etc to aid progress.

20. The Problem of GCSE Texts and Pupils with Special Educational Needs

C. Starns (1989)

Background

For Starns the problems were very different. She worked in a 13−18 Comprehensive School where she taught English. J was one of her pupils with special educational needs whom she taught in a mixed ability G.C.S.E. group. She explained the policy of the school as one where after a one year introductory course in English, all pupils undertake a five term continuous assessment course in G.C.S.E. Language and G.C.S.E. Literature. These courses are taught in a mixed ability tutor group and all pupils are expected to follow this course. It was decided that an attempt should be made through this research to make the Literature texts studied by the classes more accessible to pupils with special educational needs. For the purpose of this research one particular G.C.S.E. text, *Of Mice and Men* by John Steinbeck, was chosen as a typical text for mixed ability English.

Starns (op cit) described J in these terms:

> J was fifteen years old and had always lived and attended school in the town. He lived in the poorer area with his father who was unemployed. He was the youngest of four, the three siblings being female. J was rather small in stature and dressed rather scruffily, often wearing a tee shirt in the middle of winter. His father was always willing to contact the school by telephone or note about how J had been treated at school and his absences although he never attended parent's evenings.
>
> J was a relatively popular pupil with his peers and was pleasant on an individual basis with staff. He showed a willingness to please but was usually unable to find the determination to stick to his aims.
>
> J was timetabled for three hours per week in English lessons with his tutor group of twenty-seven. He was also one of twenty-two pupils in his year who followed an Integrated Studies course instead of choosing options. On this course he had some extra tuition in English skills and took the A.E.B. Basic test in English in May of his final school year. His timetable consisted of twelve half hour Integrated Studies lessons, six Maths, six English, five Art, five CDT, four Modern Science and two Games, each lesson lasting for half an hour.

Before being able to assist J with his English it was important to gain an overall view of the problem. This involved looking at previous research done in this area.

Although the G.C.S.E. is a relatively new area, some research had already been published on the problems pupils with special needs may experience when following a G.C.S.E. course. The six examination boards set up a working party to look at provision for these pupils. Their aim was to enable all pupils to show the skills acquired by compensating for pupils with limitations without giving an unfair advantage. Therefore physically disabled pupils can use technical aids but pupils with low reading ages cannot have examination questions read to them and the question cannot be explained. It is also possible for other provisions to be given by a Board upon special application by a teacher although this is on the basis of a doctor's or psychologist's report. In real terms, this means that nothing can be done to prevent a pupil like J suffering in examinations where he cannot read the question and therefore cannot show his understanding of the subject. A course that is graded solely on continuous assessment obviously eliminates many of these problems. However they must still be borne in mind when timed and unaided papers are set.

Williamson and Williamson (1986) looked at the language used in the sheets given to pupils to follow in lessons. They examined recipes used in Home Economics and discovered that even simplified versions were often couched in obscure terminology. Having used readability tests to find the reading age level of recipes they discovered that in spite of short sentences and some words appropriate for a low reading age they often used jargon terms, assumed previous knowledge or abbreviated instructions. In tests they proved that longer explanations that described clearly what pupils should do, clarifying the order in which steps should be followed and omitting jargon terms wherever possible, were much easier for pupils with reading difficulties to use unaided. It is therefore vital that these findings are recognized when assignment sheets are written for G.C.S.E. work. It is also useful to remember that a readability test may be of some help as a rough guide to the standard of language of a literature text but it cannot be relied on totally. The teacher's own judgement of content is equally important.

Thus it can be seen that the writing of assignment sheets for pupils with learning difficulties is a very important factor in determining their final grade. However for pupils who have a low concentration span it is equally important that the content of lessons is appealing to them.

It can be concluded from the above that the teacher has an important role in making the subject matter accessible to a pupil with learning difficulties. The first step in the action research was therefore to observe J to discover the exact problem the teacher researcher faced and then to plan actions on the observations.

Action Research

The first step in the action plan was to observe J's behaviour during the reading of the text and record his behaviour. The following table shows his behaviour over a ten minute period before lunch:

TIME	BEHAVIOUR	OBSERVATIONS
11.40 am	Stares straight ahead.	Despite J looking around the room it is apparent from his expression that he is listening until almost the end of the reading.
11.41 am	Glances out of window, yawns.	
11.42 am	Looks at book cover, talks to friend, looks round room.	
11.44 am	Picks fingernails, looks out of window, looks at his watch.	

11.45 am	Head in arms. Teacher reminds class of place in text.
11.46 am	Follows in text, yawns, looks at book cover.
11.47 am	Looks into space, back to book cover.
11.49 am	Looks around room and at person reading.
11.50 am	Looks at watch.
11.51 am	Plays with book, lines up fingers and eyes as if shooting. Yawns.

It is interesting that he never once stayed still for longer than about thirty seconds. It was also interesting that when the relevant place in the text was indicated to the class, J immediately went back to his text as if he wished to follow (although not for very long!)

The teacher researcher undertook a similar observation the following day, recording the length of time J spent on each of his actions and the results showed a similar lack of concentration.

The next step in the research was to involve J in a full class discussion of the opening of the novel after a reading of it. He took an active part showing good immediate recall and demonstrating that despite appearances he had been listening to and absorbing the reading.

Having read more of the text, the whole class were divided into pairs to play a game of 'verbal tennis' on the two main characters. J was working with a pupil of similar ability and was able to show good knowledge of character during the few moments he was observed. He also appeared to enjoy the game. When the class reading of the novel was finished the video of *Of Mice and Men* was watched. Although he was only present for half of this he clearly recognized where the film differed from the novel. J was observed whilst watching the film, as the following table shows:

TIME	BEHAVIOUR	OBSERVATION
9.30 am	Watches screen.	J display a slightly longer concentration span when watching the video although his attention still wanders more
9.32 am	Talks to neighbour.	
9.33 am	Looks behind him.	
9.34 am	Talks to neighbour, watches screen.	
9.36 am	Yawns.	

9.37 am	Glances around the room.
9.38 am	Watches screen, glances at watch.
9.39 am	Whispers to other neighbour.
9.40 am	Returns to screen.

frequently than most pupils'. It is interesting that he persistently returns to the screen but is unable to do this when reading the novel.

It became clear that his main problem was lack of concentration. He could spend only a very short time on one event before being distracted. From previous lessons it was known that he could get very involved in a piece of work and so got upset when he lost work — which happened frequently. At other times he was quite happy to waste a whole lesson by finding a variety of excuses. This was true of all his subject areas except drawing.

The final task before writing an assignment was for the class to be divided into mixed ability friendship groups of about four pupils. Each group was given an essay title and plan and brainstormed for half a lesson onto a large sheet of paper which was then shared with the whole class.' He was orally very active during this lesson and produced some excellent ideas although he refused to do the writing or to present the groups' ideas to the class. During this exercise he was frequently led into irrelevant conversation by others in the group and also disrupted the group himself and often had to be reminded of the task in hand.

At this point the class started to write the assignment in class individually. This was the stage where J faltered. Having planned the essay with his group, the teacher discussed his work with him and orally he was very accurate. However, whenever he was left to work alone he was distracted and wrote very little on his paper. His work was kept for him as he had a tendency to lose work. In the second lesson his behaviour and achievement was much the same as in the first. The support teacher came in to help him in the next lesson but he was absent.

After this, J was out of school on a two week work experience placement. When he returned he had lost the notes he had taken with him to work on (at his own request) and the class had started work on a playscript. So he managed not to produce a piece of written work to show his understanding of the text.

After his work experience, it was possible to spend a whole lesson alone with J discussing the text. He had enjoyed the novel, in particular having it read to him. He liked the main character and enjoyed the more violent scenes although he had preferred reading *Kes* by Barry Hines the previous year as it was about a 'kid', not grown-ups.

A section of the book was read to him and J answered detailed questions on the passage. He then read a section aloud quite competently. The only word he didn't know was 'morosely'. It was interesting that he often said 'What does that say? Is it . . .' and then read it unaided. He found the names difficult but managed eventually to read them. He even managed the rather difficult dialect. Afterwards he orally answered questions on the passage he had read. In a general discussion of the text it became clear that he had excellent recall of a novel read to him a month previously.

Later J revealed that this was the type of story he would choose to read. He said he didn't read books very often but he sometimes read *The Daily Star*, the free newspapers, computer magazines and motor cross magazines.

Whilst J was on his work experience it was necessary to make G.C.S.E entries for pupils. After much deliberation, it was decided that he could not be entered for G.C.S.E Literature as he had not completed enough assignments and could not realistically hope to do so. Thus, he would concentrate on G.C.S.E Language in his final term.

Outcomes

Starns argued that the initial steps taken in the action plan were obviously helpful to J as he was able to show his involvement in the text and take part orally.

She continued: 'It is important to analyse the reasons why the work was not successful for J and to outline possible steps forward. The main factor contributing to his inability to complete work would appear to be absence from school. From school records it is evident that this Spring term J has attended school for fifteen out of the possible twenty eight school days, and thus eight of the seventeen English lessons.'

That school year, J attended just thirty-three one hour English lessons. Understandably for a pupil who has a short concentration span this will lead to much disjointed and unfinished work. It was interesting to see how little English tuition statistically each pupil actually receives. The problem with this would appear to be that when a pupil misses a lot of school for whatever reason (illness, work experience) it is almost impossible to catch up in the lesson as the pupil will have perhaps missed a section of a novel, or the preparation for an assignment, as when s/he returns the class may have started a new topic which they need to discover. For a very able pupil or one who likes to work at home this may not be too difficult, but the majority of pupils do not fit into these groups.

One way to overcome this may be to use a support teacher to help a pupil to catch up. However, there was only one support teacher available for five English classes so they are often in demand and there is also a problem, as seen earlier, that the pupil might be away when the support teacher is available. As the booking has to be done in advance it may mean the pupil returns for one or two lessons before working with a support teacher, leading to further problems of inconsistency.

Another solution to this problem would be for each pupil to work on an individual programme at their own pace for the duration of the course. However, on a practical basis this would take a lot of teacher time to organise. Also in English a text being read to the class together is as important an element of the course as is group and class discussion. This would not be possible if all were working at different stages.

A second possible contributing factor is the task itself. J can work well, as has been seen, when something really fires his interest. For example, he completed an excellent project on his work experience in Integrated Studies as it was an area he thoroughly enjoyed. Thus, in future it may be more profitable for pupils to have more of a say in the type of assignments they do and the literature they study although as stated before it would not be possible for all the work studied to be on an individual basis. This would echo the aims of the Records of Achievement process. J may have had more success working from an article in one of his magazines although clearly this would not lead to a high literature grade in terms of G.C.S.E, but would enable him to obtain a suitable grade for his ability.

The next possible factor to be considered was the actual task sheet. As the article by Williamson and Williamson (1986) suggests, the sheet may have been unhelpful. Before any more assignments are tackled it will be necessary to examine and re-write the sheets in a more clearly defined sequence.

J was actually able to start his essay. The final hurdle at which he stumbled was completing the essay, a problem he had experienced in the past. It was departmental practice for pupils to commence work in class and then finish at home for homework. Clearly this was unhelpful for J as may be the case for many pupils. It would perhaps be worth altering the procedure so that reading/preparation or copying up work only is done at home and all the writing is done in class. This would, of course, mean providing possible optional work for pupils who would inevitably finish several lessons before the slower workers. This would need to be tried to see if it would work in practice. Many pupils may take advantage of a system that was prepared to allow them as much time as they wanted to complete work.

The final contributing factor was the stage in the course at which this research was started. It would probably have been more successful if implemented at an earlier stage so he would have been able to at least complete a written task. His withdrawal from the course made this impractical.

Conclusions

This research proved very valuable to the teacher researcher. The work done highlighted how little time in terms of hours in class there is to complete a G.C.S.E course. It also showed how easy it is for any pupils to fall behind in course work through absence for whatever reason. Lessons are almost never repeated and therefore even a visit to the dentist may lead to an assignment not being completed and yet 100 per cent attendance cannot reasonably be expected from any pupil. It is therefore vital that every teacher plans and structures his/her lessons in such a way that absences do not detract from a pupil's learning. It is also important that schools provide facilities so that pupils may use and listen to videos and tape recordings to catch up where appropriate and that they provide a clearly explained assignment sheet to every pupil so that it is not necessary to explain an exercise individually to twenty six pupils.

From the research it became clear that mixed ability classes cannot be taught by one process with varying tasks at the end. Each pupil's needs must be catered for at each stage which means the teacher must be flexible. For example, some pupils may wish to discuss their ideas in pairs, some may wish to play a game such as verbal tennis, whereas some may want to write down their ideas. It should be possible for each to choose the method best suited to them.

The most fundamental issue raised is that to help solve a pupil's problem it is vital to discover the exact nature of the difficulties. J did not complete literature assignments but his problem was not that he could not read or understand the Literature. His problem was a short concentration span curtailing the time available to complete work. In future, J must be given a very short section of work to complete and a clear but reasonable time scale in which to work. He cannot conceptualize 20 assignments in two years but he can tackle three lines of description in fifteen minutes.

It must always be remembered that every pupil, every problem encountered and every solution may be different. This may appear at first very time consuming but in fact in most cases solutions will not take long and should actually save the teacher time in the end as endless explanations and discipline problems are replaced by clear worksheets and interested, involved pupils whose individual needs are being catered for.

In summary, this action research cycle should be attempted with any pupil who is not achieving so that pupils can take a more active role in their own learning and teachers can expect to achieve a higher level of success.

21. Peer Tutoring

D. Turner (1990)

Background

This research developed the work undertaken by Major (1989). (See Chapter 1). She pointed out that:

> The school had for some time had problems with lack of parental involvement and an increased need for support for reading.

A paired reading scheme had been proposed and a questionnaire drawn up to obtain evidence for parental support. This survey indicated:

> a picture of deprivation, a lack of stimulation in the home, lack of parental co-operation with school and low aspirations for the children.

As a result of this research, an allowance of £600 was made to the school to set up a paired reading approach in the summer of 1989. Turner was to implement the scheme with her class of twenty-eight seven to eight year olds whilst monitoring the progress for this action research cycle. Unfortunately the money allocated for this project did not materialise until late January of that school year. It therefore proved impossible to have sufficient time to study the effect of 'Paired Reading' in time to meet the network deadline.

However, whilst expecting the imminent launch of the scheme she had embarked on a system of peer tutoring using Year 6 juniors (ten to eleven years) as tutors and Year 3 juniors (seven to eight years) as tutees.

Action Research

The peer tutors were to listen to the tutees reading during four afternoon breaks (approx 40 minutes per week). In a class of twenty-eight seven to eight year olds, eight had been classified as children with specific learning difficulties. All had reading ages between six years and six months and six years and nine months.

The tutees originally had a selection of books to choose from to read to their tutors. The tutors and tutees were matched for a relationship to develop and had a simple checksheet to fill in.

There were some difficulties when the tutors were involved in Christmas activities and when the flu virus hit both tutors and tutees at different times. One of the tutors had a long absence. However, replacement tutors were found. Some of the tutors found it difficult to monitor how well the children understood what they had read. A new more structured approach seemed appropriate. The Ginn reading scheme with activity sheets was adopted. This proved quite successful with both tutors and tutees enjoying it.

Research evidence indicates that peer tutoring can be of benefit to both tutor and tutee by making learning more efficient and pleasurable for the tutee and increasing significantly the learning of the tutors. For example, it has been suggested by Topping (1987), that tutoring can 'reconcile traditional and progressive approaches to education, making it possible to combine intellectual structure (the strength of the former) with a socially pleasant experience (attraction of the latter). Further it can give tutors the opportunity to care for other people, offer flexibility to teachers in mixed ability classes and ease the strain on teachers.'

Outcomes

Turner found that the scheme was impeded by the unreliability of tutors and the timing as most of the tutee group were boys and some of them began to resent giving up a playtime.

Of the eight original tutors only three attended regularly but each of these children felt that both they and the tutee had benefited from their time together. One pair in particular helped the tutee who had been very difficult to begin with. She would often refuse to read and deliberately make it difficult for the tutor but gradually she began to enjoy the attention and the praise. The teacher researcher believed that the change for the better in this child's attitude can be partly attributed to the relationship that was built up between these two children. Another tutor felt that she had gained more patience and become less angry with her younger sister. The third tutor had enjoyed helping and expressed a feeling of satisfaction that the boy she had helped had improved. The children were tested after approximately three months of peer tutoring and their results indicated a good improvement in this period.

Turner used a running record form of miscue analysis on each child at the start of the scheme as it was too difficult for the children to attempt a straightforward miscue. She decided this after the first child tested scored 50 per cent incorrect responses. After three months she tested him again with the same piece of work with a score of only 10 per cent incorrect responses.

	1st Analysis	*2nd Analysis*
A	20% I.R.	8% I.R.
G	33% I.R.	20% I.R.
B	30% I.R.	10% I.R.
M	10% I.R.	1% I.R.
D	12% I.R.	6% I.R.
J	8% I.R.	0% I.R.
C	10% I.R.	6% I.R.
S	31% I.R.	18% I.R.

Table 1: Results of two tests based on miscue analysis

Turner points out that she could not be sure that the improvement in the children's scores had been aided by the peer tutoring or whether it was just a natural progression. Certainly the child who had the most constant tutor achieved a remarkable change in behaviour. However, her results were not as high as some of the others. Overall, the children made improvements of between five and twelve months in their reading abilities from September to March.

Conclusions

Experimenting with peer tutoring in this way led to a more frequent use of such techniques in the classroom. For example, when a pupil understood a concept in mathematics or science they tried to teach it to another pupil. The children enjoyed using their learning to benefit others and it was found that it freed the teacher to concentrate on other tasks.

22. An Apparently Reluctant Reader

J. Holland (1991)

Background

S was born in July 1984, the third child of a family. The eldest sibling was a girl, the second a boy. S had no abnormal medical problems, except for a lazy eye which had earlier received hospital attention. S always came to school neatly dressed and appeared to come from a caring family. S entered the school via a nursery school, and a playgroup. The family had recently moved into the area. She had had several changes to contend with as a very young child. The cumulative experience of such changes could have caused stress through mechanisms similar to those outlined by Bowlby (1990). This element will be referred to later in the study.

An earlier nursery report noted that S was timid, anxious and shy in new situations. It was also reported that S had poor relationships with both her peers and adults. In addition, some lack of gross and fine motor co-ordination was noted.

S joined the Year 2 class in September 1990. She was at first quiet and unsure. Many children take time to settle in a new class. S was, however, towards the extreme. In contrast, her peer relationships did seem normal. There were two classmates in her inner social group. S came to the class with a reading book. This was at the Gayway introductory level. She had no word or letter sound recognition and her writing was at the 'underwriting stage'.

In these respects she was performing at the level expected of a reception rather than a Year 2 aged child. However, in contrast, S did seem to be 'reading ready'. She was very articulate, she could match and sequence, and had a fair memory. In addition, her comprehension levels were high, as were her hand-eye co-ordination.

She was one of the better painters and sketchers in the class, and her letter formation too was good. It was troubling that she was not 'assembling' these skills, and in contrast to most of the class, she did not take her book home to read. Most of the class were always keen to seize any opportunity to have a one-to-one read with either the teacher or a helper. S, however, never asked to read.

Considering that it has long been argued that the prerequisites of reading include not only skills and knowledge but also attitude, S did not seem to have a 'good' attitude towards reading. Her number skills too were not at the level of her peers. She had low conservation of number, and needed the support of a 'number machine' to undertake even very simple additions. This again was more like a reception child than a Year 2 child.

S's previous teacher confirmed these findings. She had been 'behind' and reading had been a particular worry. The teacher felt that, as with many children, reading would 'click' into place with maturity.

A learning support teacher had seen her in the previous Spring Term and had been equally puzzled as to why she was not making headway. An intervention programme was devised in the areas of reading, writing and number work. S received a short period each day with the welfare assistant. The support teacher in the Autumn Term was also puzzled by S and her inability to make progress. The support teacher concentrated on S and another child during her two hourly sessions with the class each week.

Just before the Autumn half-term, Holland contacted S's parents. Her mother came into school and was obviously very anxious about the whole situation. She felt that S was feeling 'pushed out' by her younger sister and was gaining attention by refusing to read. The teacher researcher suggested that, for the time being, S should not take her book home.

Hewison and Tizzard (1980) contend that parental involvement is the most important factor in children making reading progress. However, for S, parental involvement seemed to be a negative factor.

Shortly after the visit by mum, there was a strange incident in class. S came to the teacher in tears with her 'word tin', saying that she did not want to take it home. This came as a complete surprise, since she had not been given one. Investigations revealed that the word tin had been provided by her previous teacher. The incident with the tin, together with her reluctance to take her reading book home, and her mother's perspective on the problem, seemed to point to an anxiety component in the problem.

Chazan (1989) found that fear and anxiety appear to be fairly common in children up to five years of age. Perhaps around ten per cent of children of this age could be described as 'timid'. Most children grow out of this condition, at least to the extent where it does not unduly affect work.

It was claimed that parental involvement was crucial in overcoming this problem. Parents, with much contact with their children, are in an ideal position to deal with this through a mixture of positive reinforcement, shaping and ignoring. Anxieties have multiple causes, and there could well be a personality component. Perhaps the move that S had experienced when younger had contributed towards the anxiety? Perhaps it was just her nature? It was possible to speculate, but not identify the cause.

By the Autumn half-term, there had been some progress in S's number work. She was now recording simple additions and had also been using the School Scottish Maths Scheme. She had been weaned off underwriting and was not using a word book, although she still received quite a lot of support. For example, she could not find pages in the wordbook herself. S did not use 'finger spaces', and needed the page marking where she was to start the next word.

By December, S knew thirteen words, and six sounds. Progress had been made, but at a very slow rate and well below that of her peers. Most of S's peers could write at least with minimal help; some could now write several pages. All but two of her peers were past the Green Level Gayway Stage, and some had progressed beyond Orange Level. There were some other children in the class making slow progress, but they lacked the general alertness and awareness of S.

In December. this teacher researcher brought these issues to the Action Research Network for fresh ideas.

Action Research

Several useful strategies were suggested. One was that S could well be bored with the Gayway scheme after several terms of 'failure'. It was suggested that she changed to the Fuzzbuzz scheme. This idea was pursued through the learning support service and shortly after Christmas S began the Fuzzbuzz scheme. There was general consensus in the Group that in this case S reading to her parents was highly likely to be a negative element, and thus should cease.

Other suggestions raised at the Network meetings included peer tutoring. One concern with this suggestion was that S, being 'bright', was aware of her problem and to be coached by a peer may have lowered further her self esteem regarding reading.

Holland spent one month each side of the Easter holidays on secondment. During this time, S was tested by the Learning Support Service using the Aston Index and the Salford Sentence Reading.

Outcomes

The results were confirmation of previous thoughts. S had a vocabulary scale two years above her chronological Age. Her mental age was six months above her chronological age. However, she knew only half her initial sounds, and the Schonell spelling test had to be abandoned as she became stressed.

Her visual sequential memory, both pictorial and symbolic, were lower than expected for her age, as was her auditory sequential memory. She had no capability at all of sound blending but was aware that print carried a message. In conversation, she said that her mother read to her, but father did not like reading.

It was thought that S had both a block through fear of failure and also lacked some sub-skills. A paired reading approach was suggested, though this may have perhaps been more appropriate as her vocabulary increased. Perhaps significantly, just two days later, S asked the learning support teacher if she could take her book home.

During the next few meetings of the group, various other suggestions were made. One included using a 'Breakthrough' type approach to help S with her writing. This would mean writing the words she wanted on cards. She could then place them in front of her during her writing, hopefully this would make copying easier.

S was asked if she thought this system would help, and she said it might. This system was introduced using words on cards. First S thought of a sentence, it was then checked that she had the words. Holland wrote out any new words. S then copied the sentence and drew her picture.

S seemed far happier with this system than using her word book. She had also enjoyed making 'fun sentences', having a good sense of humour. S then actually asked if she could write a sentence, and would sometimes write up to three small sentences each day, usually funny ones. S also started taking her word card envelope home to show her mum. Other suggestions included the use of the 'PITCH' programme, a 'games with parents at home' approach.

It was also suggested that the mother came and helped in the classroom, though she had not been keen on this previously. Another suggestion was to try the computer with the Concept Keyboard. S was one of the few children in the class who was not keen on the computer, and it was thus not a motivator.

Conclusions

The objective measure used in the study was the number of words S recognised. Her ability to recognise words was tested at approximately three week intervals, and plotted. In terms of overall progress, S greatly improved. When she came into the class she could only recognise her own name.

After the start of the intervention, however, the rate of increase was initially maintained at about the same rate. After four months, the graph did show an acceleration, which was maintained for a further month. The increase could be related to the intervention, though even if this was the case, it was not possible to untangle which of the main two strategies made the difference. Nor was it possible to predict whether the rate would increase, decrease or remain constant.

Another measure was that of her general attitude to reading and writing. Before the intervention, she seemed to have a negative attitude towards both reading and writing. She was neither keen to read, nor to take her book home. S would thus at least passively avoid both reading and writing. The change to the Fuzzbuzz scheme did seem to catch her imagination, and she now had a far more positive approach towards reading and writing. S even started to ask if she could show her Fuzzbuzz material to the rest of the class, and even read aloud to her peers, with help.

This was a dramatic change of attitude. Thus, although attitude is a subjective measure, Holland felt that this had become positive towards both reading and writing. Both the change of scheme, and the lack of pressure in taking her book home helped, but so too had the sympathetic support she received.

With regard to writing, S seemed to enjoy a little writing and reading when combined with a lot of drawing and colouring. Such assessments of 'attitude' are, of course, subjective, as opposed to the more objective measure of word recognition. However, she contended that the change in attitude was highly relevant. S became a lot more relaxed about reading and writing, and started making progress. For the short time that S remained in the class, Holland continued with the Fuzzbuzz Scheme and emphasised the fun element of reading, which hopefully was reinforced at home. She also helped S establish a basic sight vocabulary by introducing the Hull Basic Sight Vocabulary.

With regard to home, both parents were seen at the end of the year, and it was suggested that they continue reading to her, rather than listen to her read. The parents were still very concerned about the situation, and the teacher researcher stressed the importance of making reading a 'fun thing', and avoiding putting pressure on S, however well meant. In addition, when S was ready to read to her mother, a 'paired reading' non-threatening approach would be emphasised.

After the learning support teacher had tested S, it was suggested that a psychologist become involved, and a formal assessment seemed to be the next step. Techniques such as family therapy may have been relevant, and a more precise identification of the problem obtained.

One of the main issues that emerged from the study was the difficulty in adopting a 'true' scientific approach in the classroom. The classroom is not a laboratory, and there are a multiplicity of variables that affect the situation. It is difficult to postulate a cause for a problem and to identify and thus evaluate the effects of interventions on that cause.

One general conclusion was that parental involvement in reading may not always be a positive asset. This is in direct contrast to the generally accepted view. Another conclusion was that motivation and attitude are important in the learning process. This idea is of course in line with generally held views.

Another lesson was the value of sharing a problem. Outsiders to both the class and the school can offer new perspectives and mutual support. The process of analysing the problem, and justifying actions to 'outsiders' as well as challenging personal assumptions is at least marginally threatening, but a valuable process for self development.

23. Teaching a Child with Specific Learning Difficulties in a Comprehensive School

M. Hall (1990)

Background

T came to a large comprehensive school having previously attended five other schools before the age of twelve. His parents chose this school as it had a special needs unit attached and they felt that this would be the best place for him. Because of reorganisation and the integration of special needs pupils into mainstream, the unit no longer exists but T still has the continued support of specialist teachers both in-class and on a withdrawal basis. His parents were very cooperative and were quite anxious about their son's learning difficulties.

T was a child who had been statemented and therefore had already been identified as having learning difficulties. He was being assessed by an educational psychologist at the Dyslexia Clinic. The conclusion was that T suffered quite a severe degree of specific learning difficulties. This related to areas of reading, spelling, maths and handwriting.

In finding out more about dyslexia, Hall found the following points useful. Firstly the auditory dyslexic may show no progress on standard word reading tests which demand phonic analysis. Contextual clues from a piece of prose may be easier. Further, the visual dyslexic tends to miss double letters and misspell words containing *ea, ai, oa, ew, au, ough, igh.* Possibly alphabetic spelling alongside kinaesthetic learning is the answer, linking words with visual units together e.g. 'I eat beans with my meat, I eat great meals'. Lastly, emphasis should be placed on writing as much as possible with constant reinforcement and over-learning when necessary. Word structure, spelling rules and word derivation are studied.

Information from the Dyslexia Institute indicated that some 4 per cent of children are dyslexic and that this is a congenital disability. Research indicates that in order to read well a child needs good auditory and visual perceptions and good oral and manual kinaesthetics.

In order to help such children, a multi-sensory approach must be taken. This should include visual, auditory and manual dexterity and a structured programme for reading and writing letters and words.

Action Research

T was unable to recite the alphabet all the way through at the age of twelve. He also had problems with short term memory (e.g. repeating a number sequence, repeating a sequence of letters). Not surprisingly the output of written work was small. T also suffered from medical problems. He had a mild hearing loss and had grommets inserted at the age of five and suffered from hay fever in the summer months. Other tests and observations showed that he confused *b/d* and was below average in visual sequential memory which had hindered progress in reading and spelling. His sound discrimination was slightly below average, therefore limiting sequencing and recall. Finally the analysis indicated T had a weakness with vowel digraphs e.g. he had written 'year' as 'yer' and 'dream' as 'dram'.

Hall indicated one further problem, which had not been highlighted by the consultants' reports, that of anxiety. As his teacher she stated, 'I was in a better position to observe and diagnose the problem which had to be resolved before any meaningful learning could occur. I became aware that T was showing signs of anxiety'. The following observations were made over the first few weeks in her school.

He was reluctant to read and he assured me that he had read nearly all the books that we had. He was reluctant to write, he was extremely slow at getting the smallest piece of work recorded. He was reluctant to draw. He told me that one teacher at a previous school had actually torn up a drawing that he had done. He assured me that he had done a number of the SMP maths booklets at his old school which happened to be a middle school. He would yawn frequently when asked to read or to tackle a mathematical problem.

As T was a child of average intelligence who was very articulate, eager and chatty, it was possible that he had given the appearance of coping with work at his previous schools and had therefore missed out on continuity of specialist help.

Hall comments, 'My aim was to give him plenty of confidence, enough to recognise his problems, not be afraid of making mistakes and to work together in order to cope with his difficulties ... the curriculum could be approached with fun but also must be seen to be purposeful.'

A multi-sensory approach was to be taken and T was integrated into the mainstream school for as many subjects as possible. Care was taken to counteract any labelling as a 'remmy' by other children in his tutor group. His form tutor was very aware of the dangers which could befall a child in his situation and monitored his progress with care.

Hall continued:

T and I talked about the tests that he had undertaken at the Dyslexic Clinic and he said 'I spent hours and hours on tests that day and I am really fed up with them, I don't want to go through all that again.'

She agreed that too many tests could be boring and concluded that she would have to be careful about assessment. In any case it required an educational psychologist to carry out certain tests and she would use other means of checking on what lines of action should be taken. In the circumstances she felt the most appropriate approach was the Special Needs Action Programme's (SNAP) basic skills check-list. She pointed out that the use of this checklist produced a dilemma for her as it was not designed for children diagnosed as suffering from a Specific Learning Difficulty and the boxes should only be ticked off when the child had mastered a skill. However, she felt the most appropriate approach here would be to use it to indicate where T could master the skill.

Outcomes

An analysis of the check-list pointed to the need for further action with reading difficulties. The check-list showed that he read phonically regular words e.g. 'moth', 'dash', and had difficulty with 'magic *e*' words. Similarly he showed difficulties reading words with common vowel digraphs. Beyond this he also needed to over-learn new words and there was need for more work on punctuation.

His maths work showed considerable need for help with basic skills. This was particularly the case with his subtraction of two figure numbers, multiplication tables and division, where clearly he had little idea of the concepts involved.

In order to help him, Hall used the following strategies. For reading development, T had explained that he had already experienced paired reading but said that he was a bit fed up with it and didn't want to carry on at home with mother, (even though she was very conscientious in carrying the practice out). Hall stated, 'that was alright at the moment (which was the beginning of the academic year), but that we must still read.' She continued:

> I did not restrict his choice of reading material but he was still reluctant to read. Talk, yes, read no! T would begin to yawn as soon as we started reading. (I suspected, bearing in mind the point made by Cotterell, 1985, that this had become an automatic response now to any reading), but he would attempt to use decoding skills and contextual clues. I would encourage him to sequence from left to right.'

For his spelling the emphasis was on trying to improve. Hall comments: 'I used the 'Look, cover, write, check' method that Cripps and Peter (1991) advocated: in a reading session I would pick out three words from the text he had difficulty with and he would write them in his book. This would be done employing the multi-sensory approach: eyes/ears/voice/hand. She also used a structured approach similar to 'Attack' but had to present it in an interesting, 'fun' way, using words from the topic area or studying a situation that was found relevant.

Finding words within words, letter strings, alphabet games, splitting words into syllables were the strategies used. Attention was drawn to spelling rules and these were kept in a book. He had his own spelling directory. He learnt how to do neat joined writing and was very proud of it. Lined paper was used.

Computer games were used to help him and 'Folio' for writing. He was encouraged to write short passages which would then be checked for mistakes. These would be highlighted and discussed. Hall reported that this had met with moderate success. These passages would be corrected and simple rules of punctuation and grammar would be discussed at this time, although he still experienced difficulty in this skill. A future resolve was to make sure that he did at least one small piece of free writing every week whilst making sure that some form of written work was undertaken every day.

T had difficulties in understanding basic concepts in maths, yet had been put on a Secondary maths SMP course at his former school. T said he had covered a number of the booklets already. It soon became evident that he would have to embark on a course which went 'back to basics'. In order to make an assessment of T's needs, Hall used the basic skills check-list. From the evidence it was obvious that there was a great deal of ground that needed to be covered.

Fortunately, Hall was able to obtain the help of an advisory teacher in mathematics who suggested that it might be useful to use the new SMP scheme for slow learners, which was still in draft form. This had been produced by Sheffield Hallam University with the help and advice of teachers.

The scheme was designed and produced in the same format, i.e. booklets on themes, as the SMP used in mainstream. Slow learners would be familiar with the layout and format of the scheme and it seemed ideal. Pupils could easily link in and follow the scheme throughout the lower school, thereby allowing for continuity. T also used taped SMP booklets based on work carried out by another member of the Action Research Network.

Conclusions

Hall summed up her experiences stating:

> One of my aims was to get rid of the anxiety displayed by T. It is certain that there has been success in this area. Allowing him to relax and removing competition which has been achieved by placing him in a small withdrawal group for some of his lessons, and helping him to recognise and cope with his difficulties has had positive results.

This observation was supported by his parents who were relieved to have had some of the anxiety about T's learning difficulties taken from them. They had felt guilty about being constantly on the move when T was young. His mother had joined paired reading schemes run by different schools and would conscientiously carry this out but she had observed that T was getting fed up with it. They had dropped it for a while and mum still felt guilty at not carrying it out. She was reassured when Hall said she would be able to concentrate on his reading for a while and then, when T was ready, perhaps she could occasionally read with him.

Further there was an improvement in T's reading and he started to volunteer to read aloud in front of a small group, whether it was in French or English and this could be taken as pleasing evidence of some progress.

His handwriting was very good but there was enough evidence from the analysis of the data that there were many areas in mathematics and language work that needed continued specialised support even though there had been some progress made.

One future strategy would be to help T develop note taking skills in order to help him integrate more into mainstream classes.

24. Classroom Strategies for Poor Spellers

S. Stothard (1990)

Background

This action research project was described as follows:

> I have encountered many children from different schools and backgrounds who have a spelling problem. It would seem nearly every class has a group of children who come under the umbrella of 'poor spellers'. Even when a school follows definite spelling policies and strategies aimed at giving the children a method of approaching spelling, there always seems to remain a small number of children who cannot or are reluctant to break through the barrier into the world of spellers.

She decided to observe and monitor such children and follow their spelling progress with the hope of finding some answers.

The school already had a good whole school policy and strategy for spelling. It followed the 'Look, cover, write, check' method described in Cripps and Peters (op cit). This was reinforced by use of a word pattern book; an exercise book in which double pages are folded into eight columns. The first column is left empty so as to become the cover flap, the second column is used for the word. This can be any word misspelt in a story. The child then looks at the word and folds column one over column two and writes the word in column three. The word is checked and if correct then other words with the same pattern can be added to the page and a pattern label added at the top right to enable a child to easily find this pattern. Should the word be wrong the child looks again, covers the word, and writes it in column four and so on.

When writing, a child is encouraged not to stop and check a spelling as this will lead to a break in the flow of ideas but simply to underline a word that they are unsure of or unable to spell and then check and find out when the written work is completed.

For most children these methods of approaching spelling work well. But on checking through a previous class's summer spelling scores it was obvious that for a small group of children these methods were not enough.

Action Research

> In September, once my class of first year juniors had had time to settle, I decided to test their spelling ability and find out which children had particular problems. I used the Spar Spelling Test as it is both easy and quick to administer. Using the results I took the four children with the lowest scores and followed their progress through a series of spelling situations and monitored their progress.

In September the group were all seven years old and the tests indicated that they had a spelling age about one year less than this. Having chosen the children it was now time to consider the approach. Stothard had already spent some time reinforcing the 'look cover write check' method, and as a class had talked about taking a magic photo by looking at a word, keeping its picture in mind and then being able to write the word from memory. However, a close look at the group's written work indicated that this was not enough.

Below are two transcripts of some written work done by D and B without any help (the words 'guinea pigs' and 'Thistle' were given). The story was about the class guinea pig, 'Thistle', who had recently had three babies.

D wrote – Thistle had 3 beeabs nawe wiee hath 5 beabee we a note kidgee the beabe case ther culur is blac and chineg mistr goslin mede a huche.
(*Thistle had three babies, now we have five babies we need another cage – the babies cage. Their colour is black and ginger. Mr Gosling made a hutch*).

B wrote – The guinea pigs was don on Wesday and the guinea pigs ore
little and the guinea pigs ore drown and whitit we bw nt to
cllu them. I Im then tinn a name forr them and the pigs ore
Nis The pig Tissl This some twe babies.

(*The guinea pigs was born on Wednesday and the guinea
pigs are little and the guinea pigs are brown and white we do
not (know what) to call them. I'm thinking (of) a name for
them and the pigs are nice. The pig Thistle (had) some three
babies.*)

An analysis of their spellings using the Spelling Diagnosis Sheet C
(devised by the local support service) was conducted. There were a few
reversals e.g. *born = don* and a few words that could be the result of
auditory perception and articulation *now = nawe*. However, the
majority of spelling errors were reasonable to unreasonable phonic
alternatives. The words that were causing problems were everyday
words that most of the other children in the class seemed to have
mastered in their story work.

From these results, Stothard felt the basic class approach was right for
these children but didn't go far enough; these four needed a more
structured and individual approach. Two of these children at times
found self-organisation difficult, e.g. could never find a pencil at the
start of a lesson etc.

She decided to focus spelling effort on a core of commonly used
words some phonically regular and a few useful irregular words so that
each child could build up a core of 'everyday' words that they were able
to spell and felt confident about writing. At the same time she wanted to
reinforce their visual memory approach and their familiarity with word
patterns.

Having looked at several lists of key words and spelling lists, she
decided to use one which was ordered into common, regular and
irregular word groups. The class were divided into several groups
according to need and she set up weekly lists of ten words. The four had
a total of five irregular words and five phonically regular words a week
to learn. Ideally, it would probably have been better to select words as
they arose in their language, but in terms of management this was
difficult and very time consuming if it were to be a class effort. It was
important not to isolate these four children from the class and show
them up to be such poor spellers that they needed special treatment.

All the words were taken home and parents asked to support their
children in this method with these words. The children were encouraged

at school to use them orally and discuss their meaning. Most weeks they were given opportunity to use the computer – a program called 'Starspell' which helped them to reinforce the pattern work and visual memory. Although they had five irregular words at the end of a week, the first word in the list was omitted and a new irregular word added so that these words were learnt and reinforced over five weeks. Meanwhile a new phonic pattern was looked at each week. The work on the computer seemed to them to be fun not 'work' and it proved to be a good motivator.

Outcomes

Each week the class had a spelling test. All the words that the four pupils had 'learnt' were logged and the whole class was given a dictation which contained the words that these four children had in their spelling lists. The dictation contained fifty words. The results showed that girl A achieved 70 per cent correct while Boy B managed 54 per cent. Boy C got the best score (82 per cent) while Boy D managed 64 per cent.

It was now six months since the first Spar Spelling Test and so they were retested again. This showed a big improvement in attainment. A had improved by twenty months during this period, while the boys had improved only slightly. Boy B improved four months, D some three months and C showed no improvement at all.

The words were checked on the Spar Spelling Test against those in the weekly list. It was found that those words worked on were spelt correctly in the test but the words they had not looked at had caused problems and had been substituted by a reasonable phonic alternative.

These results left Stothard with a number of unanswered questions. Was the Spar Test inappropriate for these children? Was the criterion reference testing approach using the dictation and the weekly words a more realistic way of assessing their progress? Should she expect these children with learning problems to be able to generalize their learning and add words to their core of spellings without a structured approach at this stage?

She felt it would be useful at this time to get the children to do another piece of free unaided work. The locality had recently experienced severe gales and so the children wrote an imaginary or factual story on this topic. On examining their February stories and comparing them to their October stories, she felt there were definite indications of progression.

Finally, it was decided to assess their attitude to spelling and see how this fitted into their individual spelling performances. These results were most interesting. With hindsight she wished this aspect had been checked earlier. She devised a spelling questionnaire and everyone filled it in supposedly truthfully and honestly. The result of this indicated the following:

Child A who had shown the most progress revealed herself to be a concerned speller who thought she was a poor speller but always tried. She thought that weekly lists, tests and pattern books helped.
Child B who had made minimal progress did not worry about spellings. Even though he thought he was a poor speller he only worked hard sometimes to learn words but he liked having tests and using the word pattern book.
Child C who made no progress on the Spar Test, thought he was a very good speller and never worried about spelling words but enjoyed the tests and word pattern books.
Child D always worried about spellings and always worked hard to improve but still thought the tests and pattern book work helped.

Having considered these 'attitude questionnaires' it was felt they were quite a reasonable and accurate reflection of the four children involved.

Conclusions

From the results of this research, it was soon obvious that for these children spelling was not an isolated problem but just a part of wider learning problems which included attitude towards learning, concentration and poor language skills. Stothard also indicated that the results of the attitude questionnaire provided an important key to each individual child's problem. A who was concerned, tried hard, recognised that she was poor at spelling and made the largest amount of progress (20 months on the Spar Test and 78 per cent in the dictation). However B and C didn't really worry or consider they had a particular problem with spelling and only made minimal progress on the Spar Test, (B four months, C stayed the same). In the dictation, B scored only 54 per cent whereas C scored 82 per cent. The results for C did tend to be erratic and she felt this related to his work patterns in class. D had a good attitude and worked hard but needed a very structured approach moving at a slow pace to suit his ability.

She felt perhaps it would have been useful to have had a greater emphasis on promoting a better attitude for these children with learning problems so as to enable them to use the spelling methods within the classroom. Time to talk to such children individually in a counselling way would seem well spent if it could be afforded.

Further she felt that motivation was another area closely linked with attitude to learning. She noticed that on occasions when Child C and D shared story writing using the computer as a word processor, there were far less spelling errors. They were far more inclined to discuss with each other whether a word looked right or not. They seemed to look at their writing as a reader would whereas when working in their own book, checking work and drafting seemed a painful chore to them. Beyond these points, she also felt that the computer program 'Starspell' was very useful as a friendly reinforcer of word patterns and visual memory work.

Finally, the use of structured word lists and weekly tests did at the very least focus attention on word patterns and learning methods. It gave an awareness of spellings, and she considered it was this basic process of looking at, thinking about, and wanting to spell a word correctly, that was needed to go alongside the spelling methods encouraged within the classroom.

25. Teaching Joined Handwriting to Five Year Olds

P. Williams (1989)

Background

Williams introduced her work in the following terms:

> In the course of many years' teaching experience with junior aged children with learning difficulties, I began to feel that it was possible that some of the problems they had with spelling and the perennial problems with reversed *b* and *d* and inverted *u* and *n*, which resisted attempts at remediation, could be more closely connected with faulty letter formation than with perception problems.

This led her to think whether the practice of teaching children to print, rather than write, was partly responsible for this. She argued that individually printed letters in a word have no direct physical relationship with the letters on either side of them and it seems illogical to insist that, for example, to write an *a*, start it like a *c* then carry on round to the top and put a stick down the side. Further, she pointed out the objections to this type of instruction, even if it is accompanied by a demonstration, are that in the first place the child has no real point of reference for beginning the letter. If it is going to end up looking more or less like a circle what difference does it make if the circle is drawn in a clockwise or anti-clockwise direction and does it matter if the 'stick' is put on the left or the right hand side, or if it is drawn from the top to the bottom or vice-versa?

From the point of view of spelling, many people, notably Peters (1985) and Cripps and Peters (1991) are of the opinion that not only is spelling a visual skill, rather than an auditory one, but it also depends to a great extent upon the mechanical repetition of certain letter strings to which the hand becomes accustomed and which one learns to write automatically with very little thought. Logically, if these strings are written in one continuous flow then spelling them never presents any difficulty, 'ough', 'ing', 'ie', 'and' are examples which immediately spring to mind. Most adults write 'ie' automatically and have to stop to think about the exceptions after 'c'.

Having considered these points in relation to junior aged children, Williams began to think about the accepted practice of teaching infants to print, and to wonder whether there was any sound educational reason for doing so. It did not seem to be sensible to teach a technique to children at the age of five when they are possibly at their most receptive age and then, two or three years later, to virtually tell them to forget what they have learned and do something different because they are now old enough to 'do joined writing'.

From further reading, mainly the work of Jarman (1979) and Sassoon (1982), she discovered that children have not always learned to print. In 1913 Johnson, who had been investigating old manuscripts and penmanship in the British Museum, suggested the form of the Roman alphabet which became known as 'print script' in an attempt to make life easier for five year olds who had to struggle with the copperplate writing originally intended for the Civil Service, along with pointed steel nibs and watery ink. Anything which gave relief from this latter system was almost certain to be greeted with open arms by teachers. By 1916, most London schools were teaching it and its use gradually spread through the rest of the country.

Unfortunately, as has been pointed out, the hand movement encouraged by printing can lead to disjointed, disconnected movements. Letters which are built up in a 'ball and stick' framework of separate units contrasted with the natural flow of scribble seen when pre-school children 'write' and which with training can lead on to a legible, fluent and fast hand, can be inhibited and frequently lost, not always being recovered when joined handwriting is eventually taught.

Action Research

These thoughts were discussed with the local advisers for English and special educational needs and, with their support and encouragement she decided to carry out an investigation into the feasibility of teaching reception class children to write, rather than print, right from the start. She comments:

> Since I do not work in one single school and do not normally have access to reception class children, my first task was to identify schools where the head and staff would be willing to take part in the project. Initially I intended to use one school, but the English adviser suggested that three completely different schools might provide more reliable information. Consequently, I approached various headteachers and, without too much difficulty, identified three who were willing to participate.

Having obtained the co-operation of the headteachers, a meeting was arranged for all the teachers involved. At this meeting initial issues were discussed.

It was decided that parents should be informed of the decision to teach joined handwriting at meetings held in the term before the children were due to start school and that in the case of two schools, she would go to the meeting and talk to the parents about the reasons for doing the work and about the thinking behind the decision.

It was felt to be unlikely that early reading development would be adversely affected, since all children are surrounded by different types of print and writing in their environment, e.g. labels on food stuffs, television adverts, letters arriving in the home, and the different writing styles used by parents, grandparents, playschool and nursery school teachers.

Since the school was to have ownership of the project, each one had to be free to choose what was considered to be the most appropriate style. In the event, each school chose a different style, one opted for the Fagg R style another for Jarman's Basic Modern Hand and the third for a version of Marian Richardson, which would be adapted to include an open *b* and *p* and a looped *k*. The re-writing activities were to be done related to the normal activities involving paper, paint, sand, and pattern making.

A host of questions arose. For example, would differences in the teachers' handwriting, which would inevitably arise if a uniform style was adopted, have an adverse affect on the children? It was felt that this would be unlikely, as similar differences would occur in printing. What would be done if the children appeared to be suffering or 'losing out' in any way? The general feeling was that this was unlikely, but everyone was prepared, if necessary, to admit to having made an error of judgement and to abandon the project since all that would be necessary would be to simply drop the joins and revert to teaching in the traditional way.

Other important decisions had to be taken. These included a policy on notices and captions. Here the decision was taken to write, not print, any names, notices around the classroom or captions under work. There was no question of work cards or previously prepared equipment being altered or amended as it was felt that this would make the whole project into too much of a burden for the class teachers.

Bearing in mind the importance of all writing developing from the child's felt need for communication, it was decided that the first words the children should be taught to write would be their names.

Notice was also taken of the fact that, because of the early admissions policy in operation in the schools, several of the children would only recently have had their fourth birthday upon entering school. This was not seen as presenting any particular difficulty, since every child would be treated as an individual and would only be expected to move from stage to stage when ready.

Because of the constraints imposed upon time by other commitments, Williams was in a position where she could only arrange to visit each school once a week for an hour each time. This, although not satisfactory, was the best that could be done at this point.

It was decided that her role should be to act as a co-ordinator and liaise between the schools, to provide appropriate materials where available and to disseminate any knowledge or information that might come her way in the course of reading from books and journals. She also decided that she would take part in the actual teaching that went on during her visits, fitting in with whatever activity the class teacher felt was appropriate.

In addition, it was decided that the easiest way to evaluate and decide upon future tactics would be to hold a short 'post mortem' at the end of each session to consider whether things had gone well or badly, to consider strategies for the following week, bearing in mind that learning to write would be an ongoing process not limited to one hour a week, and to discuss ways and means of overcoming specific problems which might occur, as well as looking at whatever might have gone particularly well during the week.

Also a meeting of the whole group would be held once every half term to discuss progress and, if possible, to consider a specific topic connected with handwriting. It was felt by everyone that the main task of the group at these meetings would be to support one another in their uncertainties, and to discuss future strategies.

Outcomes

Work on pre-writing activities designed to develop motor and visual skills began as soon as the children entered school. As would be expected, the children were all at different stages of development ranging from those who clearly had no experience of handling paper, pencils and other similar materials, to others who had already begun to make attempts at writing and at writing their names. In one way, the latter children caused more problems than the former. Those without previous experience had no preconceptions about writing and the way in which letters should be formed, whereas some of the others had already learned to form some letters sometimes incorrectly, which meant that bad habits were already becoming established.

Two examples will illustrate the range of ability and experience that were found. D could not hold a pencil and was totally incapable of following a left to right movement across the paper with his finger even when guided by an adult. A could 'write' his name, but he used a mixture of upper and lower case letters, incorrectly formed, and insisted that his way was correct because it was 'what Mummy had taught him'.

D's problem was relatively easy to solve. A car driving game was invented. A set of tables was completely covered with large sheets of taped-together kitchen paper and various obstacles, such as bricks and small containers, were placed on the paper at intervals of about a foot. A cut out model of a car was attached to a thick felt-tipped marker and D was shown how to 'drive' the car round the obstacles, the felt tip leaving a trail on the paper which he could see. His first two or three attempts ended with him 'crashing' the car, but he soon grasped the idea and was able to move from left to right, avoiding the obstacles completely. Once he had acquired this skill, it was possible to transfer it to ordinary sized paper and pencil.

A proved to be rather more difficult, because the teacher did not want to undervalue what he had learned at home, but he obviously could not be allowed to continue forming letters badly. By a process of telling him frequently that it was very good that he could already write, and that his writing was very nice, but that now he had come to school things were done a little differently, he gradually came to accept the idea of writing a different way and made good progress!

Each school had a slightly different approach to the actual teaching, but common to all of them was the emphasis on drawing, painting, pattern making, sand-play and, slightly later, writing patterns based on straight lines, top to bottom movements, flowing patterns which led on to joining strokes and so on. All the time the children received constant praise and were encouraged to take pride in doing something as well as they possibly could. By Christmas, a large number of the children could make a good attempt at writing their name, many of them unaided, and even the ones who had appeared to have great difficulties were making progress in holding pencils correctly and in general motor control.

Some reservations were felt about the fact that, in one school in particular, the children were slower in beginning to produce their own free writing and were relying for longer on their teachers to write for them. This was discussed at a weekly 'post mortem' and it was decided that this probably did not matter, since all the children were being given plenty of opportunities to develop their language verbally and to record in ways other than writing, such as painting.

By the mid-point in the project the more able children were starting to copy words and sentences written by their teachers and one or two were trying to write sentences unaided. It was interesting to note that two girls in particular tended not to join their letters until they were reminded to do so, when they reverted to joining without any apparent difficulty.

At this stage, it was also realised that despite careful teaching and constant demonstration, some of the children were forming letters incorrectly. In order to overcome this, one of the teachers decided to try 'talk and chalk' lessons. These were kept very short, no longer than ten to fifteen minutes at a time. Each child was given a chalk board and a coloured chalk. The teacher then demonstrated a letter on the blackboard and 'talked' the children through it while they first of all practised writing it in the air with a finger, then on the table top and then on the chalk board with the chalk. All the children, whatever their ability, joined in this activity and all of them thoroughly enjoyed doing it. In discussing this later, it was concluded that this was possibly because when children play 'school' they often have 'teacher' writing on the blackboard and that possibly these 'lessons' fitted in with their previous ideas of what happened in school.

Conclusions

The approach seemed to work and the children began to learn short letter strings based on those appearing in the hundred key words. It was decided to start with these words as they are all important basic vocabulary which the children will be able to use in reading as well as writing.

One problem that arose was that instead of writing very large letters, as most infants tend to do when they first learn to print, many of the children began to make their writing very small, much more the sort of size that an adult's writing would be. Fortunately, while the schools were trying to decide whether they needed to do something about this to prevent the writing from becoming cramped and badly formed, the children seemed to revert to large writing. It seemed that this was just a phase in their development, but it could possibly form a starting point for some further investigation along the lines of seeing whether all five year olds who are being taught to write do it, or if it was just peculiar to the children in this part of the project.

26. Active Learning Techniques as a Method of Developing Social Skills in Pupils with Moderate Learning Diffculties

S. Baber (1989)

Background

This action research study centred on learning problems exhibited by much older children of secondary school age in a special school for children with moderate learning difficulties. The investigation involved looking at a group of thirteen and fourteen year olds who experienced problems in developing social relationships and exhibited behaviour which limited social interaction.

The individuals in the group had a variety of special educational needs, ranging from reading difficulties to poor perceptual skills.

The home background of these pupils varied considerably, some children coming from a council estate in a central area of town, others living in isolated villages in outlying rural areas. Family background also differed, one pupil being fostered by his grandparents; others were from single parent families, several from large families, while others were from 'average' size families.

The behaviour of individuals within the group also differed, from an introvert who appeared totally isolated, to those pupils whose aggressive behaviour caused concern. Most of the group exhibited immature behaviour, e.g. being silly, calling each other names, lack of sense of responsibility, etc.

There was a total lack of cohesion in the group and any forms of small or whole group work were virtually impossible. Individuals in the group would work on their own but the disruption in the group meant that there were many distractions.

There were two main reasons for concern about this situation. Firstly, productivity within the group was at a very low level and individuals were not working to their full potential. Secondly, these pupils would be leaving school in one or two years time, and their level of social competence implied that they would have serious problems communicating and coping in the 'real world'.

The transfer from school to adult life is a difficult time for most pupils and those with learning difficulties find this transition particularly hard. Most of this group had difficulty learning within one situation and their transferability of skills and poor assimilation restricted their lifestyle. Through a whole staff discussion it was decided that the group as a whole needed to develop social skills in a variety of settings that would be relevant to their future lives.

Action Research

Some fact finding was undertaken into the background of this problem. In particular this was related to the concept of social skills and teaching strategies as discussed by Hargie (1989) and Hargie, Saunders and Dickson (1981).

For the purposes of this study, a pragmatic explanation was needed if the concept of social skill was to be considered within the school curriculum. The inspectorate, for example, suggested that the aims of personal and social skills in schools were:

> to meet personal needs, such as dressing oneself, handling a knife and fork, using a telephone.
>
> (By definition these can be identified as motor skills).
>
> to adjust to different social contexts; to consider others' views; to contribute, co-operate and take the lead as appropriate within groups; to accept responsibility. (D.E.S. 1985).

The LEA guidelines on this subject indicated that important skills and concepts to be dealt with included:

Self awareness; relating to others (one to one and in groups: appreciating another person's viewpoint, appreciating another person's achievements); discussing, debating, negotiating; leading and following; competing (where appropriate); helping, sharing and collaborating; evaluating motives;self-discipline (setting realistic personal goals, persevering, managing time, energy and resources); survival, which included adjusting, compromising and coping. Humberside L.E.A. (l985)

Baber argued that if an attempt to improve the social skills of the target group was to be made, two emphases must be adopted. Firstly the direct teaching of social skills must be pursued and secondly the incidental learning of social skills through everyday occurrences should be emphasised.

In teaching social skills, a variety of teaching procedures are available. For example O'Leary and O'Leary (1977) have discussed various types of behaviour reinforcement programmes resulting in a practical strategy that could be used in the classroom, viz.

1. Rules have to be applied to the classroom.
2. Rules have to still apply and the inappropriate behaviour has to be ignored.
3. The appropriate behaviours have to be reinforced while the first two strategies are still being applied.

(rules + ignore inappropriate behaviour + reinforce appropriate behaviour)

Due to the extent of the problem and the complexity of behaviour modification it was decided to attempt to facilitate the learning of social skills through teaching procedures. Of the numerous teaching procedures available, role-play was identified as the one most suitable for the task in hand. This procedure was used as the main activity within the active learning stages which were used as a structure for the lessons. Four weeks were allowed within the school curriculum to implement the planned strategies. A developmental programme was devised and one hour per day was set aside to put this plan into action. The progression within the programme meant that at its inception the pupils would be working individually, and by its completion they should be confident and skilled enough to work in groups.

Two members of staff would adopt behaviour modification techniques applied during trial lessons, i.e. the learning outcomes and rules of the lesson would be discussed with the group at the beginning of the lesson and these would be written on a blackboard and stay there throughout the lesson. Undesired behaviour would be ignored and as much positive reinforcement as possible would be used to reward appropriate behaviour.

A number of situations were listed that it was felt the pupils had experience of or would encounter in their lives. These situations varied from those involving only one person, to group activity, in which each member of the group would have to undertake a role. The action plan included working individually, in pairs, and in small groups as they progressed through the programme.

The data was collected using several methods which included:

group discussion and review, observation by teachers, discussion and review by participating teachers, notes on individual pupils' responses and behaviours, and evaluation of each lesson set against objectives and prescribed outcomes.

Outcomes

An initial reluctance by some group members to take part in the activities suggested a lack of confidence and fear of embarrassment. It was also possible that the lack of understanding of the relevance of this work on the part of individuals was a contributing factor. Sometimes just the fact that an activity is 'new' can prevent pupils from performing, as they are unsure of their capabilities in unknown situations. On the other hand some pupils exhibited immature behaviour, taking the whole exercise lightly and 'fooling around' or being over-exuberant. These behaviours were used as a learning exercise and most of the first lesson was taken up as a debrief or discussion, talking through some of the exhibited behaviours and why people behaved in such a way. The discussion examined people's different perspectives of given situations and people's feelings.

During subsequent lessons more care was taken in the introduction, and the lesson objectives were discussed with the whole group. A warm up activity was used to get the group 'in the mood', before the theme of the role play was suggested. This approach created a climate more conducive to the main activity and more pupils entered into the exercises on the second lesson. Though this lesson as a whole was assessed as not being a success, set against the prescribed outcomes, some individuals in the group achieved some of the objectives. This success was positively reinforced by the staff and the successful work was used as an example or model for the rest of the group. Again the second lesson was debriefed and discussion around the set situation was expressed as being 'fruitful'. Every opportunity for positive feedback was given to the pupils.

Early indicators suggested that discussion was more successful than role play, but this seemed to be dominated by several pupils and allowed some group members to only have passive involvement. The first week of the programme did not achieve the planned scheme, but it was felt that a great deal of learning, for both pupils and teachers, had resulted from the lessons which had included the social skills needs in talking to different people, for example friends, parents, teachers, shop-keepers, etc.

An evaluation of this first week's programme led the planning of the ensuing weeks to be more structured. During the second week it was planned to get the pupils working in pairs on given situations. These situations were well structured and written so that each group had a card. For example:

> You want to go on a school trip but you cannot afford to pay for it yourself.
>
> | | |
> |---|---|
> | Place: | Kitchen in your house |
> | Time: | After school |
> | People: | You and one of your parents |
> | Relationship: | Son/daughter and mother/father |
> | Problem: | You want your parent to let you go on the trip and pay for it. |

It was obvious, by the willingness of the group members, that individual confidence was growing and during the second week everyone entered into a role play situation. The majority of the pupils were now obviously enjoying the activity and this was expressed by the quality of work that was being produced by some and the interest shown, at the end of the lesson, as pupils asked what they were going to do in the next lesson.

Certainly the relevance of the work was identified particularly during the debrief sessions with comments from pupils like:

> I never thought of it like that before.
> That's what it's like in our house.
> I like doing this because it's about me.

As the small group work developed, it allowed more 'freedom' for the teachers to help the members of the group that had difficulties or needed attention to keep them on task.

Although the level of involvement and degree of achievement

increased during the programme, conflict and personal differences were still a feature of the group activity, though the frequency of such outbursts was much reduced. One of the benefits of the programme was evident when some of the more aware group members were able to suggest topics and situations that they would like to explore and discuss.

During the debriefing phase the teacher researcher was able to evaluate the activity that had been undertaken and through this it was possible to draw from the group individual social skills that they could work on and practise. An example of this is shown with listening skills, where people's behaviour can show that they are listening. These skills were identified and practised as separate activities.

As the programme progressed it was found that one situation led to another and the scheme was not followed in the third and fourth weeks, but each lesson was evaluated and the following lesson grew from this. This led to a more coherent programme than just a number of disconnected activities.

The themes that were explored in these role play lessons were expanded in other areas of the curriculum, and the role play was used as a stimulus for practical maths, life skills, writing (letters, forms, etc) and the opportunity to practice the learned skills on trips into the community (shopping, information seeking, etc). By the end of the programme an integrated approach to the curriculum had developed, and the identified role-play lesson was only a part of the work that was going on in the classroom.

A feature of the programme was the attempt of the teaching staff to offer positive reinforcement for desired behaviours and ignore undesired behaviour. Though the latter was difficult and sometimes impossible, certainly praise for expedient conduct had beneficial effects and as the group's confidence grew it became easier to use. From the teachers' point of view this exercise raised awareness of the positive and negative reinforcement that was a feature of all their contact with children.

Conclusions

The action research confirmed that the careful selection of objectives in relation to the individual or group needs was paramount. The outcomes and objectives of this programme not only gave pupils aims for their work, but also gave the teachers a list of criteria against which it was possible to measure the success of the lesson/programme.

Conclusions drawn from the programme suggested that all the group had benefited from the role play and discussion exercises, in that they had developed and practised social skills that would help them in their social interactions, and that the group as a whole had learned to work together in a more productive way than had previously been possible.

A limiting factor became apparent during the programme, in that social skills are a product of both cognitive and behavioural skills, and while it is possible to see and assess the behavioural aspects of the work, the limited cognitive function of most of the group prevented adequate decision making skills. Therefore while the skills were being developed in the structures created by the teachers, the individual pupil's ability to transfer those skills into situations in which they had to decide what to do was restricted.

This programme would have to be continued over a longer period of time, with the pupils given opportunity to use their skills in a variety of realistic situations.

Throughout the programme the opportunity for discussion and the positive feedback that was given to the pupils was seen as reinforcing learning and setting norms that they were expected to work towards. It could be argued that the expectations of the teachers and of the pupils themselves rose through the programme and this linked with success provided key motivators of learning. However, pupils with moderate learning difficulties rarely have realistic expectations of their capabilities, and 'failure', in their eyes, in real situations could prevent the adequate use of these learned skills.

One effect of the programme, was the way the pupils enjoyed the lessons after the initial fear. This had an important motivational effect which was transferred into other lessons. This led the teacher researcher to think more about the methodology used in 'traditional' lessons.

27. Colour Matching, Recognition and Labelling

K. Kent (1988)

Background

This action research was undertaken with an infant age child in a special school. It concentrated on the acquisition of the concept of colour. The teacher research comments:

> Colour is around us — it is something so familiar that many of us take it for granted. It is part of every child's environment and because of this many children do not have to be taught to identify,

name and match colours. A problem occurs when a child fails to learn these in the normal way. In this case the teacher has to start training the child in this early language development skill before she can proceed with many other areas of learning. Objects have a definite shape, texture and movability and so they can be explored with other senses as well as sight. You cannot feel, smell, taste or move colour, it is only a visual property of an object with no tactile clue to its identification — this in many ways makes it a very difficult concept to develop for children with special needs.

The Nuffield Maths teacher's handbook states that by noticing and talking about relationships which are well within a child's understanding, powers of observation are improved — e.g. 'my coat is red', 'that shoe is red', 'the flower is yellow' etc. These experiences, whether incidental or structured, form an important part of the development of both language and mathematics. The teacher needs to think about the relationships the child is to encounter and to provide situations in which they may be found and utilize these to begin to develop the visual concept of colour and then the ability to match and name colours.

The S.P.M.G. Infant Mathematics teacher's handbook states:

the concept of colour as a property of things is quite a difficult concept for some young children. Every opportunity should be taken to check on individual children's understanding of colour. A good experience is to make collections of red things, blue things and so on. Children could be given outline pictures or shapes to colour; rubber stamps or stencils could be used and a spirit duplicator could give the sample colour, e.g. colour different football jerseys. Following these experiences and the use of colour flash cards, children should gradually get to know, at least orally the words red, blue, green and yellow.

The work of Piaget (1952, 1958), Vygotsky (1962) and Bruner (1966) indicated that the development of both language and concepts are interwoven. It is impossible to teach such concepts independently. They are developed through an individual's ability to generalise on his/her experience. Thus the teacher plays an initial role in this development by providing suitably selected and arranged experiences which will enhance this process.

Action Research

The pupil at the focus of the study was statemented and a summary of this indicated that although he was a socially affectionate child, he had delayed development in all areas with more specific problems with fine motor control and speech and language.

The planned programme was undertaken over a period of seven weeks during the Easter Term. During the first week the colour red was to be introduced. From the long term observations already available to the teacher researcher it was decided to improve the child's attention span for a learning task — tasks to be given on a one-to-one basis with many changes of approach; to break down the learning task, at first, into carefully graded steps; to make each step simple enough for the child to succeed when making the response; to have achievable targets for the child; and to make provision for reward and reinforcement through praise and encouragement, but also with intermittent use of other rewards (e.g. musical clown).

It was considered important to produce experiences where the child was actively involved, this included the use of toys, games, stories and a computer. Further, it was thought important to involve over-learning by constant reinforcement throughout the day and the week. This had to be achieved without reducing enjoyment and motivation — and, therefore, would be pursued through reinforcement activities with the normal integrated topic approach, so that activities and materials used were meaningful and important.

The plan of action was directed at helping him to recognise and name the four base colours — red, green, blue and yellow, by the use of an objectives based programme. This was to be reinforced during the day within the topic based part of teaching and by the use of a variety of resources. This was to be undertaken at least eight times each day.

During week two, the knowledge of red was to be reinforced while the experience of yellow was introduced, on a similar basis to that outlined above for red. Week three was to be concerned with the reinforcement of both red and yellow. By week four, the experience of blue to be undertaken with the reinforcement (on a lesser scale now) of red and yellow. Week five was to be concerned with all three colours and week six with the experience of green. The last week was to be directed to the contrasts between blue and green.

Outcomes

Kent reported that things did not go to plan. The plan of action ceased after week three because of absences by the child.

A diary of the project was kept, however, and this indicated some measure of success in the period. This showed that failures occurred as the teaching periods came to an end due to the failing concentration of the child. Failure also increased as another colour was introduced.

However, as the new colour was reinforced at periods during the day, the rate of failure decreased.

It was also observed that better results were achieved when there was a strong motivating factor – musical clown, sweets, necklace to be worn – this also worked to improve attention span. Beyond this, other points were also made clear. For example, concentration was less when in a group situation e.g. games, music, stories because of distraction of closeness of peers and in games and music because there was a time lapse between the child being actively involved.

The child became far more confident in both matching, recognising and labelling colour as the number of reinforcements increased.

The failure rate increased in the third week when two colours were introduced together (red and yellow) – the action plan was changed here and red and yellow were reinforced for a second week The resulting success rate was far better suggesting that because there were now two colours, more reinforcement was required. Spontaneous use of colour names increased in this final week.

Conclusions

Kent concluded that learning increased as the task was broken down into carefully graded steps. Attention span increased with praise and increased further with knowledge that there would be an intermittent reward. The child's attention span increased when actively involved throughout the activity and the success rate increased as reinforcement increased throughout the week. A longer period of reinforcement was required as more factors (e.g. two colours) were introduced in greater proportion.

There was a constant need for language with the activity in order to associate name with colour – success of recognition of colour increased with the use of colour name by the child. All the reinforcements (experiences) used must be within the normal working model of the class – must not be contrived – and are therefore more meaningful activities for the child. When the reinforcement ceased because of absence, failure increased. These factors pointed towards the need for home/school liaison and as the failure rate increased towards the end of the activity with consequent loss of concentration and motivation, there was need for more changes of approach and tasks.

28. The Development of a Ten Minute Programme for Daily Use to Improve the Auditory Memory Skills of Infants

J. Riley (1991)

Background

Riley working with the same age range but in a mainstream infant school took a key feature of the work undertaken with that age group: that of developing the auditory memory of pupils who had been shown to have difficulties in that area. She commented:

> As a primary school teacher, part of my curricular responsibility is to administer the six-plus screening programme. The LEA recommends a ten minute daily programme of remediation to improve auditory sequential memory skills which play a great part in developing fluency in reading. I used the test results of the children in Year 2 to select the candidates for my research. I decided that I would use music rhythm patterns to help the children to remember sequences and also to focus their attention.

Action Research

The research project was described as follows:

> The ten children who scored between 0 and 2 on Test F (Auditory Sequential Memory) came to me for preliminary work for ten minutes a day for one week. This helped to settle them into a routine and to iron out any teething troubles − for instance the order in which they sat, which made a difference to the speed of recording their responses.
>
> I explained to the children why we were doing the exercises − that it might help them remember letters and words better and also make their eyes move along from one line to another more quickly in their reading books. They agreed that they would like to improve their reading and seemed to take the exercises quite seriously, (although they were fun to do too).

After the first week Riley's timetable was disrupted due to staff illness − and then came SATs. when the programme had to be abandoned for several weeks. On resuming the programme it was decided to put the children in two groups, seven from one class and three from another. This made things easier as the staff concerned allowed her to use their class support time. (Previously she had taken the children into the Hall straight after lunch, when the noise of the kitchen staff washing up and clearing away was not conducive to good concentration! Now she could use the staff room where it was quiet).

She made a simple record sheet which was easy to use and clearly showed the progression of each child. She put the names down the side and the exercises along the top. There were ten sessions altogether. They took longer than ten minutes at first, but gradually speeded up.

The programme was based around the following exercises:

1. Clapping hands together four times and slapping knees four times to establish a rhythm. Say '1, 2, 3, 4, 1, 2, 3, 4, . . .'
2. Clapping hands together twice and slapping knees twice. Say 1, 2, 1, 2, 1, 2'
3. Sing 'Twinkle, twinkle little star' whilst clapping rhythm two.
4. Days of the week − clap hands once slap knees once. 'Mon-day, Tues-day, etc'
5. Grid of 16 squares, (figure 2). Star in each square. Teacher taps under each star with rule. Children follow with eyes and clap.
6. Cover three stars (not on top line). Each child to clap (or make a sound as a variation) and rest on blank squares. (This way you can check whether they are following and making L to R movements with eyes).

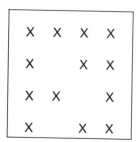

Figure 2. Example of Grid.

7. Vowel sounds − four of each on each line. Child to say aloud. Teacher taps sharply to keep rhythm (not pointing).
8. 'Football Clap'. Altogether twice then each individual. Teacher claps in between each child. (She gave it this title because it fired their enthusiasm!)
9. b, d, p, d − four of each on each line. Child says aloud (taking care not to add 'uh' to each sound), teacher taps.
10. b, d, p − mixed − sixteen grid. Each child to say. Teacher taps.
11. th, ch, sh, st. four of each on each line. Teacher points and taps.
12. th, ch, sh, st mixed. Each child to say. Teacher taps.
13. Memory recall − four words, e.g. fruit, furniture or toys. Individual response.
14. Memory recall − four numbers. (Increase these if achieved).

The reason she chose phonic exercises for most of the grid work was because these children needed phonic skills reinforcement. With younger children she would have used musical symbols/sound shapes in the grid instead. (A 'Turtles' grid was used as a reward for sitting still at the end of each session).

Alvin (1976) states that the interpretation of a musical symbol is 'reading' and that the sense of achievement and improvement in social status is immensely important in child development. Aspects of language development, such as phonics and pronunciation can also be improved.

Outcomes

1. S (a boy who possibly had specific learning difficulties) had great problems remembering sequences, for example recalling all the days of the week. An improvement was observed towards the end of the ten sessions. He had difficulty distinguishing between b, p and d when in mixed grid and could only manage half of the 'football clap'. His auditory recall improved by one from four words to five. His recall of numbers was higher in score as he was particularly keen on number skills and was anxious to excel in this exercise. The rhythm work improved and there were twelve exercises (not counting the memory recall) his score increased over the ten sessions from 3/12 to 8/12.

2. L F (a boy who was lacking in confidence and having limited memory recall), did very well from the beginning, improving his score from 9/12 to 12/12. His recall score improved from three words to a fluctuation between four and five words, the numbers being more easily remembered – but not exceeding six.

3. C (who was attending speech therapy and displaying auditory imperception of the letter e) improved his score from 7/12 to 12/12 but could not remember more than five words in the recall section, although he had no difficulty remembering 7 numbers.

4. L J (a boy with very limited language skills, hearing loss and poor co-ordination) enjoyed the sessions tremendously and his score improved from 0/12 to 4/12. Recall of words fluctuated between three and four but his number score improved from three to a general four and a final six, (although this last one may have been a lucky guess!)

5. R (a boy who displayed poor concentration and memory skills) improved his score from 6/12 to 11/12. Memory recall of words limited to five – he had no difficulty with number recall.

6. S (who had difficulties with co-ordination, speech, sight, hearing

loss, concentration poor) although phonic and reading skills were quite good – fluency and co-ordination/rhythm were poor. Score improved from 3/12 to 5/12 and memory recall fluctuated between three and four at the beginning and rose to between five and six at the end, although five words was the maximum.

7. H (the only girl) – with poor auditory memory skills improved her score from 2/12 to 11/12 out of sheer determination. She could not, however, remember more than four words in sequence, although number improved from three to six.

8. D (who had poor language skills, memory phonics and co-ordination) improved his score from 3/12 to 7/12 and his number recall from three to six – words remained at four, however, an improvement of one.

9. P (who had poor concentration and a poor self image) improved from 6/12 to 12/12, his recall score not improving at all.

10. D (again a boy with poor concentration and self image) improved from 5/12 to 11/12 (very competitive against P). His recall score did not improve, however, and fluctuated between four and five numbers and three and four words.

A table of results for the changes measured in the participating children is outlined in Table 1.

Child	General Score 1st session	General Score 10th session	Word Mean Score	Number Mean Score	Improvement of General Score	Improvement of Word Score	Improvement of Number Score
1	3/12	8/12	4–5	?–6	+5	1	0
2	9/12	12/12	3–4/5	?–6	+3	1	0
3	7/12	12/12	4–5	?–6	+5	1	0
4	0/12	4/12	3–3	3–5	+4	0	2
5	6/12	11/12	5–5	6–6	+5	0	0
6	3/12	5/12	3/4–5	4–6	+2	1	2
7	2/12	11/12	4–4	3–6	+9	0	3
8	3/12	7/12	3–4	3–6	+4	1	3
9	6/12	12/12	4–4	5–5	+6	0	0
10	5/12	11/12	4–4	5–5	+6	0	0

Table 1: Table of results achieved through the programme with all the participating children

This table indicates an improvement in the general score for all the pupils who were involved in the programme. The overall improvement in the word score was more patchy, only 50 per cent cent showing an improvement here while 40 per cent made an improvement in the number score.

Conclusions

No correlation was noted between the rate of improvement of the general score and improvement of the memory score. Suffice it to say that the programme of ten minutes a day did improve the rhythm and fluency scores of all of the children to some degree.

The activities in the programme can be varied without losing any impact – different songs, months of the year instead of days of the week, or even seasons – the Grid can be used to stimulate children's interest and enthusiasm, e.g. particular crazes of the moment, like Turtles (this was developed by using their names too – 'Donatello' etc).

Riley felt that the programme needed to be improved and perhaps a 'cue-miscue' score taken of each child before and after the series of sessions.

Part One: Overview

The projects illustrate a range of approaches to improving the learning potential of pupils with special needs. They demonstrate that with the support and encouragement of colleagues, many teachers with little or no previous experience of research-based teaching can use the outcomes of professional and practitioner enquiry to improve both the quality of their decision making and the effectiveness of their teaching.

In Part Two, the formal processes of organising such support in networks is examined in greater depth. Our purpose is to encourage critique and debate on the theory and practice of networking in the field of special educational needs.

PART TWO

School Development Through Networking

29. School Development Networking and Managing for Change

G.H. Bell and S. Dennis

The authors of this contribution were responsible for designing the networking model and they jointly present a detailed account of its development. Sue Dennis was the first co-ordinator of the networks in action. Here, she discusses their underlying rationale and anticipates some of the evaluative components that are more fully explored in the final chapter.

Background

A key issue in the development of any schooling system is the extent to which central direction is compatible with local decision making.

As the pace of educational change quickens, inherent tendencies towards the fragmentation of discourse are intensified. Innovation saturation and information overload become endemic as governments attempt to respond to the increasingly urgent need to reform, re-structure and revitalise. In this situation, the central issue for quality assurance is whether an education system is intended to transmit or to transform. In the decade ahead, particularly as the trends towards political and cultural union amongst European States gather momentum, the outcomes of this debate will be crucial to the development of inter-cultural pedagogy.

Meanwhile, as schools undertake the task of reform, the interests of special needs pupils and their teachers stand in danger of becoming marginalised. The management of change in such circumstances calls for practitioners and the agencies able to support them to organise their combined resources in a way that manages for change.

However, for this effort to be successful, experience exchange becomes a crucial necessity. Yet, certain disabling weaknesses afflict existing modes of educational discourse. Major gaps can be identified between theory and practice, research and its application, policy makers and practitioners, and accrediting institutions and professionals. As a result, current conceptions of 'professional development' and 'pedagogy' have deficits built into them on account of underdeveloped relations within and between these areas.

The central concepts of this debate have been rendered problematic because the evolution of professional status for teachers has largely been determined by agencies and institutions other than practitioners, controlled by academics and inspectors on the one hand and politicians on the other. This has meant that what counts as 'practical professional knowledge' has largely been defined by teacher training institutions and what counts as 'conditions of service' has been controlled by government, whether locally or nationally.

This situation has created barriers which need modification if not removal. The essential corrective to barriers arising from a situation in which truth is determined by who speaks and how something is said, rather than what can be justifiably sustained, is to organise professional communications in a way which both promotes agreements in judgements and co-ordinates consent. Educational discourse will thereby be transformed in favour of systematic inquiry and dialogue in which notions of truth and falsity are arrived at through the rational examination of evidence (Bell, 1985).

This requirement would shift pedagogy from 'didactics' (implying a science of teaching) to 'dialectics' (implying a science of critical inquiry). For teachers in a democracy need to be not simply technicians in the business of information transfer but facilitators of critique and dialogue. This approach will involve an active negotiation of meaning which will ensure that educating as distinct from schooling or indoctrinating arises.

Such preconditions of being an educator as distinct from a teacher, trainer or instructor also indicate a situation in which theory and practice are brought into a mutually supportive relation. But the degree of integration will depend upon certain other factors, i.e. 'that participants enter into dialogue under conditions of equal opportunity, that power relations are neutralised through an overriding aim to pursue truth, that participants have the same chance to raise issues, make proposals, call into question, sufficient to leave no assertion free from critical examination, and that discussion is sufficiently free from the distorting influence of group organisation to enable a rational consensus to emerge. (McCarthy, 1978).

In short, a system for communication in education is required which facilitates critical dialogue as a by-product of research-based teaching. Because the knowledge base to be developed is both practical and professional, it will be necessary to prefer the study of change to the study of texts, the study of cases to the study of experimental samples, and the investigation of practice to the elaboration of theoretical issues. It will also be necessary to liberate the structures of enquiry from domination by expert opinion in the interests of researchers, to participation in practitioner based enquiry in the interests of learners.

The characteristics of the knowledge base arising from such a revitalised pedagogy will result in:

- the investigation of problems and issues experienced by practitioners;
- a deepened understanding (diagnosis) of practitioners' concerns;
- explanations, interpretations and justifications provided in everyday terms;
- evidence validated in dialogue with collaborating partners;
- an ethical framework for the collection, use and release of data.

(Elliott, 1978)

A method of enquiry which attempts to meet these several requirements would be comprised of action research, case study, and collaborative investigation. 'Action research' implies planned and evaluated change with a view to improving practice, 'case study' implies unobtrusive investigation of a policy with a view to prudent judgement, and 'collaborative investigation' implies data being validated in critical dialogue with a view to audited accountability. A practitioner research approach which has been termed 'Action Inquiry' (Bell, 1988) is made up of these several elements.

The key process necessary to sustain collaborative action inquiry we suggest corresponds most closely to the idea of a 'network'.

What is Called Networking?

The central problem posed for the management of curriculum change is how teachers can gain increased access to each others' knowledge and experience. It is proposed that networking provides a solution to this problem.

In a formal sense, a 'network' refers to a coupling of nodes or points in a systematic way. In the present usage we refer to points of professional communication linked by means of a social group for social improvement. Networking in this context implies communication and partnership with a view to diffusing ideas. In classical conceptions of enquiry, notions of research, development and dissemination (R.D. + D.) describe an effort by individuals to influence policy and practice by distributing information to others. Collaboration is viewed in this system as a contingent feature. By contrast, the additional concept of 'diffusion' (R. + D. + D. + D.) presupposes information carriers operating through some principle of communication. Influence on policy or practice is thus ensured by securing the passage of ideas and information within and between centres of communication. In the former (non-networked) system, knowledge is developed and disseminated but not necessarily utilised. In the latter (networked) system it is itself a form of utilisation. In an extended 'action network' sense, (later described) information is acted upon by being utilised in situations of planned and evaluated change.

The professional communication characteristics of each type of enquiry are entirely distinct. In a non-networked R.D. + D. system there is no commitment to subsequent action or free information flow. These factors may sometimes arise but they are not formally required. In a networked (R. + D. + D. + D.) action inquiry system the presence of these factors necessarily brings about a qualitative change in the practice of participants, viz:

- a unity of purpose is secured (solidarity);
- common interests facilitate agreements in judgements (consensus);
- agreements are negotiated (contract);
- participants control the enterprise (autonomy);
- content is determined by participants (authenticity);
- outcomes are the corporate responsibility of participants (accountability);
- the division of labour is related to the agreed competence of individuals (rationality);
- values are tested in action (confirmability);
- action is subject to reflection and deliberation (critical appraisal);
- intentions and interpretations are evaluated in dialogue with participants (validation);
- the processes of engagement in networking are self educative (emancipation).

On account of these factors, action networks represent a commitment by participants to the management of change. The question then arises as to how such commitments can themselves be managed so as to overcome the main gaps identified previously as deficits in current modes of professional communication.

School Centred Action Networks

Although some researchers have identified issues pertinent to networking in the sense described above (Beresford and Bridges, 1980, Louis and Rosenblum, 1981), rarely has an opportunity been taken to examine operational issues in networking from design, implementation, operation and network change, or to examine the effectiveness of networks as a strategy for sharing knowledge and experience in order to improve the quality of teaching and learning. The School-Centred Action Network (SCAN) grew out of such concerns commencing with a preliminary survey of practitioner researchers' experience of their problem solving efforts in schools (Dennis, 1988).*

Following this survey, a Local Education Authority in England (Humberside) sponsored a co-ordinator to establish one such action network. The central question was to test whether classroom practice could be improved by making external resources available to practitioner researchers through a co-ordinated process of experiential learning. The operating hypothesis was expressed in the following terms:

If the elements of curriculum development, teacher development and information technology are linked effectively, then networking will help to remove boundaries between the elements and enhance teacher professionalism.

The networking model developed to test this hypothesis was designed to:

- organise a linkage system whereby external support including information and human resources would be made available to practitioners;
- apply research-based ideas to school problems/issues related to 'special educational needs' through access to a suite of databases provided by means of a microcomputer;

*An account of the origins of these ideas is provided in Bell, G.H. and Colbeck, B. (1989) *Experiencing Integration: the Sunnyside Action Inquiry Project,* Falmer. This project explored the concept of action networking to evaluate special educational needs policy on a whole school basis over one school year at a single site. A further elaboration of teacher based research with examples is provided in Vulliamy and Webb (1992).

— support the process of 'Action Inquiry' in which practitioners systematically identify practical problems and issues and select and implement new ideas through collaborative learning.

The project had a dual commitment to the use and dissemination of research products and to the implementation of initiatives concerned with solving school-based problems. (See figure 3)

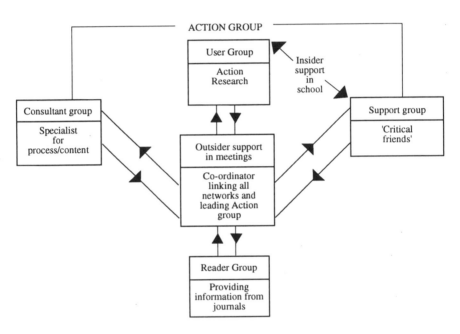

Figure 3   The networking model

The main elements of the networking model shown in Figure 3 are:

- a *Reader* group, comprising a wide variety of volunteer teachers, support teachers and advisers whose task was to abstract information from a range of journals.

- a *Consultant* group of specialists in research methodology and 'special educational needs'.

- a *Support* group of teachers who, having completed an award bearing course or one action research cycle, wished to support a new generation of Users.

• a *User* group of volunteer practitioner researchers who identified themselves as wishing to join the network by responding to an open invitation sent to all primary and secondary schools in the area.

• a *Network Co-ordinator* seconded full-time for one term to become familiar with both the workings of the network and the suite of microcomputer databases through which information flow could be facilitated. In addition, a secondment for two days per week for one year was provided to initiate and supply training for the various groups, to facilitate the processes of interaction between groups, to act as link agent between users of information contained in the knowledge base and supporters/consultants, and to disseminate research findings. As the Co-ordinator was replaced yearly, certain prerequisites were identified for the appointment of each new Co-ordinator, i.e.,

   − active involvement in action research,
   − and/or experience of being a User;
   − experience of being a Supporter;
   − agreement to become the Evaluator for the following network.

The key strategy of this networking model is that the User is active in his/her learning and is therefore able to be self-critical. Contacts between the nodes are shown by arrows, most resulting in a two way flow of information both internally and externally so that information about practice is freely exchanged. To achieve this, channels of communication are set up enabling the participants to engage in sustained dialogue about the nature of teaching and learning within the various school contexts. This includes being actively involved in negotiating processes and outcomes and in gathering and cross-checking different perspectives as a means of validating any judgements that may be reached. The work is collaborative, with a maximum flow of information between the User, Consultant and Supporter with hypotheses being openly stated as they develop.

In this approach to professional collaboration, each successive stage produces insights that reflect back on the preceding stages and suggest possibilities for the future. In these respects, the inquiry elements resemble 'fourth generation evaluation' strategies as subsequently outlined by Guba and Lincoln (1989). The networking process provides each User with assistance in the following sequence of activities:

   − identification of a problem or issue in curriculum policy;
   − examination of alternative solutions focusing on the products of relevant research provided on a microcomputer database;

156

– selection of a specific solution;
– implementation of the solution;
– evaluation and incorporation of both the solution and the problem
solving process in action steps taken with a view to improvement.

By engaging in this process of systematic self-inquiry, the Users submit their practice to critical reflection, and in this way attempt to rectify the deficiencies they identify. The process of generating grounded theory from a detailed analysis of practice is a key characteristic of Action Research, and by making the outcomes available on a microcomputer database the use of such knowledge is encouraged and its dissemination for each new generation of Users is facilitated. The diagram in figure 4 indicates the practical support provided by a suite of microcomputer data bases.

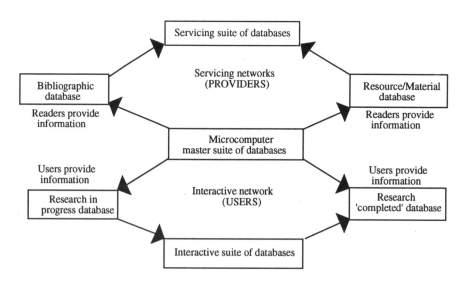

Figure 4   Knowledge base for practitioner research networks

As the diagram shows, the Reader group provides a service for practitioner researchers by processing bibliographic and resource-material information, i.e. creating a 'servicing' network. To complement this servicing suite of databases, practitioner researchers (Users) carry out action research and contribute to developing a related suite of databases by providing information of 'research in progress' and 'research completed' thereby not only using but supplying information, i.e. creating an 'interactive' network.

It was considered essential to develop the bibliographic database first because the information needs of Users involved in action research demands that the findings of existing studies are validated through the data of the Users' practice. The 'research completed' database provides a means of disseminating the knowledge and experience gained by Users engaged in action research. This is constructed from the summative reports developed at the culmination of the networking cycle. The case for computerised storage and retrieval of information within the context of practitioner researcher is neatly summarised by Stenhouse (1979), in the phrase 'using research means doing research'. Providing a knowledge base in the form of a suite of microcomputer databases meets the needs for disseminating the knowledge and experience gained and avoids wasteful overlap and duplication of research effort. The procedures for accessing the knowledge base, both provided and created, are outlined in the diagram shown in figure 5.

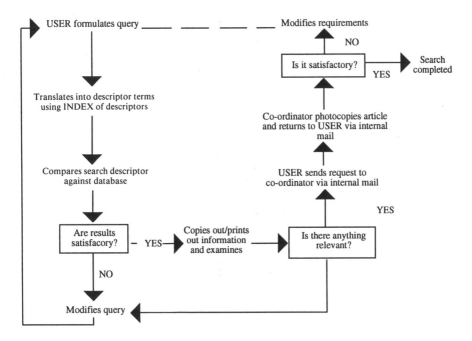

Figure 5   Typical database search

Throughout the course of its development, the aim of the system was to ensure that the microcomputer database grew in a way which was designed to be supportive and which focused on the Users. The basic idea was to provide a route for practitioners to obtain and exchange practical professional information on 'Special Education Needs'. This involved a 'bring and buy' or collaborative principle, which was proposed as being a precondition of making networks work in practice as distinct from theory.

In summary, the training and delivery components of the action can be described as follows:

- a *co-ordinator maintaining and managing services* and acting as a 'clearing house' agent.
- a *base* to house the general administration of the network, (e.g. Teachers' Centre).
- a *central collection* of bibliographic and teacher-based research information for distribution on request.

operating through the processes of:

- *resource management* including organising access to technical assistance and making microcomputer database information readily available.
- *supporting and facilitating* action research and action learning.

Managing Networks and Networking

The conditions which need to be satisfied in managing an effective network are numerous. For example, as has already been discussed, the basic process of practical knowledge transfer requires a particular form of structured communication. Whilst this condition was met through action networks, a further need was created for a service delivery and professional support function as well. The essential networking activity involved arranging task centred individual relationships and ensuring effective communication across all of the elements. Each element must function as intended for networking to work. Whilst improvements in the practice of individuals is the main criterion of success, the effectiveness of the communication process may be evaluated in terms both of the diffusion of ideas in changing attitudes and beliefs (Maude, 1974; Rogers and Shoemaker, 1971) and the uses of information in encouraging the implementation of innovation. (Bell and Pennington, 1988).

Many factors influence the ability of a network understood in these terms to function effectively. Chief amongst these factors are:

- the clarity of the goals of the network;

– clarification of the expectations and responsibilities of each component in the network;
– an explicit understanding of the nature of the services to be delivered.

In our experience, the critical steps in both network building and networking maintenance include:

– introductory activities, e.g. mobilising resources;
– securing a state of readiness for the networking components to facilitate collaborative relationships;
– co-ordinating and monitoring the network in operation;
– actively managing network change.

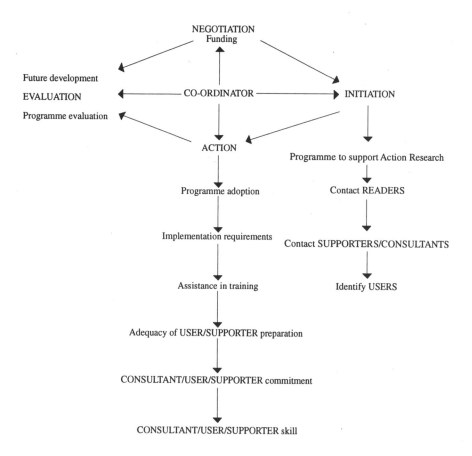

Figure 6   The four phases in network building and maintenance

The diagram (figure 6) summarises the four phases involved in initiating, building and maintaining school centred action networks. Management practices at each of these phases are affected by a number of additional factors mainly concerned with the quality and continuity of support from various agencies, e.g.

- the Teachers' Centre or similar being actively involved as host for the 'home base';
- the Supporters' commitment to the process of networking;
- The Consultants' readiness to provide additional resources and collaboration;
- the Users' willingness to investigate their own practice even if this becomes uncomfortable.

The emerging pattern of drawing upon multiple sources of information and support occurs to a large measure as a result of effectively engaging in networking activities.

Networking and the Implementation of Educational Reform

Two key questions arise from this model. Does it provide an effective tool for school development? If so, in what ways does it fit into such changes as may be required through implementing central government educational reforms?

A major measure of effectiveness is continuity and demand. If the networking model remains intact as verified by evaluation data then this may indicate a degree of client satisfaction pointing towards improved performance. Budgeting, personnel factors, cycles of the programme, organisational rules, resource distribution and the maintenance of support services are further indicators.

However, the effectiveness of the network is totally dependent on the willingness of participants to commit themselves to meetings and research processes, and to contact others in the network for assistance and information. Tentative evidence from early evaluation data suggests that patterns of communication and the exchange of information are determined by the management style of the Co-ordinator who orchestrates the activities which bring together the Users, Supporters and Consultants. Additional evidence indicates that networking adds resources, enriches the curriculum and outperforms existing practices by providing support without unrealistic cost implications, supplying training without unacceptable levels of withdrawal from school, and implementing innovation without undue pressure on teacher time.

Success criteria used to evaluate these effects have included member satisfaction with the quantity and quality of services delivered and reported perceptions of improvements in practice, personal achievement and professional development.

In order to sustain delivery of an effective educational reform programme, special needs pupils will require carefully structured teaching schedules and teachers will in some cases have to rely on alternative means of communication to supplement local knowledge in order to develop them. School-Centred Action Networks by encouraging planned and evaluated change promotes the achievement of these goals. Professional knowledge and experience is both facilitated and transferred by a collaborative process in which the key elements are trust, openness and continuous support.

Networking based upon the model we have outlined is conceived as an ongoing process, continuously encouraging collaboration and in this way is cumulative in its impact. It is therefore important to involve all those Users having completed an action cycle to become Supporters for the next generation of Users. By these means, knowledge gained is being disseminated, adapted and utilised, extending the role and responsibility of the User from consumer to provider.

In summary, networking as part of a Government, LEA or school 'family' or 'cluster' policy to support special educational needs pupils and their teachers involves the initiation and implementation of several related activities:

- designing and activating a linkage system;
- organising the use of external Supporters/Consultants;
- collecting and collating resources;
- providing appropriate training for Users;
- developing action research processes within the time constraints of a school calendar.

Conclusion

SCAN was designed to deliver three types of service to assist practitioners to improve classroom teaching and learning. The first service – the dissemination of evaluated practice, was intended to support the implementation of an action research cycle. This required assembling a knowledge base in the area of 'Special Educational Needs' to be delivered to Users through the activities of a network co-ordinator. The second service – i.e. technical assistance, was to enable Users to use specific databases. The third service – i.e. facilitation and support, centred on helping Users during the process of action research, and included the identification of a problem, the examination of alternative solutions, the selection of action steps using information from the knowledge base, and the implementation and evaluation of an action plan.

If it is accepted that all teaching and learning problems imply an insecure resource base and a demand for improved information for their solution, then practical assistance in the form of a suite of microcomputer databases can provide some support in these directions. Diffusion of information to Users in action networks and dissemination of the outcomes of intervention strategies arising secure the necessary conditions for collaborative forms of action research where the sharing of practical knowledge is the criterion of success.

The theory underlying this model of networking regards teachers within their schools as the most effective vehicle for enhancing the quality of the educational process. In this crucial respect the focus of discourse is on action as distinct from accountability. Moreover networking, and in particular school centred action networks, provide a reminder of the theoretical fact that only those directly concerned can speak in a practical way on their own behalf

30. Training and Developing Special Needs Teachers: Lessons from Action Research Networks

G.H. Bell and J. Major

In this final chapter, the last co-ordinator of the networks contributes her summary evaluation of the five networks operating up till 1991. The strengths and weaknesses of a collaborative action research model for in-service training and development are discussed and the challenges and opportunities of building a knowledge base in a European context are critically assessed.

Teacher Training in the 1990s

The twin crises of economic recession and the collapse of Communism have prompted re-thinking about the nature of educational institutions across Europe. The consequent impact on the perceived role of the teacher has implications for their training and development which have, as yet, fully to emerge. But in response to intimations of economic decline, the majority of European governments had already sought during the eighties to deploy the concept of 'school improvement' and 'quality' as an ideological tool. (OECD 1989). As a result of these pressures on schooling, Vonk (1991) considers that throughout Europe 'the training of teachers is at a crossroads'.

The debate is represented by two dominant models. The first, described as the 'bureaucratic-managerial' approach, regards the teacher as a technician transmitting prescribed information. The second, 'professional' approach defines the teacher as having an active role in collaborative planning for policy development. The content of training programmes for each of these models reflects conceptions of the ideal teacher. Such ideals can be expressed in the following typology:

- *the child oriented teacher*: emphasises child development and learning processes;
- the *curriculum oriented professional*: aims for mastery of curriculum and instructional design and related skills;
- the *technocratic teacher*: focuses on practical teaching and skills-oriented courses;
- the *social-oriented teacher*: determines the structure of courses in relation to the physical and social setting of the school;
- the *multi-versatile teacher*: attempts to combine all the above profiles.

Vonk (op cit), concludes that the successful integration of these conceptions of the teacher's role will yield a satisfactory theory practice relation. But he suggests that this will only occur when subjective theories are tested by available alternatives, when systematic and continuous reflection on acting and thinking is encouraged, and when external consultants and professional practitioners combine their resources. No particular method for achieving these features of teacher education is recommended other than a general plea for governments to create 'an environment in which teacher education and practising teachers co-operate on a professional basis.'

Mitter's (1991) analysis of European developments in teacher education identifies six determinants of the role of the teacher in the 1990's:

- the *economic* aspect, which indicates the teacher's income;
- the *social* aspect which explains the status of a teacher;
- the *formal/legal* aspect which defines the position of teachers within the administrative structure and affects the amount of their freedom (or restraint) within the political order;

- the *professional* aspect (in the narrow sense of this term), which describes the teacher's everyday activities;
- the *socio-educational* aspect which determines their place in the education system reflecting dominant expectations in a given society.

He concludes that 'the teacher's work as change agent remains high on the agenda of political educational considerations'. Again, no particular method of achieving this assumed benefit is offered.

A cautionary case history of the interplay of these forces in determining reform efforts in Europe is provided through a critique of the educational system in Greece; its experience being likened to the Myth of Sisyphus — 'an everlastingly repetitious and laborious task', (Kazamias, 1990).

The underlying political and cultural factors contributing to this Sisyphus effect have been penetratingly analyzed by Aronowitz and Giroux (1986) who claim that the 'crisis of schooling' will only be resolved by a 'commitment to developing forms of knowledge, pedagogy, evaluation and research that promote critical literacy and civic courage'. But, once more, the concrete details of what might count as the ideal 'critical pedagogy' are lacking. Such a discourse of critique needs to be complemented by a discourse of possibility. Talk of practitioner 'empowerment' as a necessary condition requires an account of the pragmatics of power in post-modern educational systems.

The complexities of empowering teachers are well described by Jones (1990) who traces the regulatory processes that have come to bear upon the figure of the urban schoolteacher in England, shaping their training and social position, and constraining their regenerative potential. The central conflict of being trained to transform whilst maintaining a base that was expected to be both humble and rigidly codified, poses fundamental problems that the 'deschoolers' were right to expose. (Illich 1973, Freire 1977)

But in the field of special needs education, as Diniz (1991) points out in his review of European developments, there have been major shifts in attitudes towards pupils with special needs albeit that there is still a considerable distance to travel for equal opportunities aspirations to be fully met.

However, he emphasises that the idea that every teacher is a teacher of special needs requires a whole school approach and he draws attention to the central importance of reviewing the school organisation, pedagogy and supporting resources in order to ensure that the best practice in mainstream policies secures access to the curriculum for all pupils.

The possibilities of effecting such change through school development planning underpinned by action research became increasingly
more apparent through the network members' experience. As Elliott
(1991) comments: 'Action research integrates teachers and teacher
development, curriculum development and evaluation, research and
philosophical reflection, into a unified conception of reflective
educational practice'.

It is this form of integration that, on the evidence of the action
networks, is the hidden or missing category of the well rehearsed
Warnock Report typology; locational, social and functional.

Lessons from Electronic Action Research Networking

As we have seen, each network is composed of *teacher researchers*,
volunteer *supporters* who agree to share their experience in eight
meetings over two terms and act as 'critical friends' after having
conducted at least one action research cycle themselves, *consultants* who
have acknowledged experience in a particular field, *readers* who abstract
material from educational journals for entry into a computerised
database, a *co-ordinator* who runs the network meetings, services the
micro-databases of action research information, and supports teacher
researchers in their schools, and an *evaluator* who has been a co-
ordinator and who conducts a summative evaluation.

The key events in building action networks can be presented in
summary form as follows:

1. Introductory session
   Action Research/Example Networking
2. Workshop introducing 'special needs' database and simplified user
   guide and index of descriptors.
3. Meeting to discuss practical problems/issues.
4. Meeting to identify action steps.
5. Meeting – progress report discussing data collected through
   action research cycle – group helping to analyse and interpret this
   data.
6. Meeting – peer validation of findings.
7. Group validation/evaluation of networking project based on
   'nominal group technique'.
8. Individual interviews/questionnaires to highlight participant
   perceptions on the network.

At the end of each network an evaluation takes place conducted by the
previous co-ordinator by means of the Nominal Group Technique

(Delbecq et al 1975). The resulting lists of strengths and weaknesses are prioritised by a simple voting procedure and used to implement changes in the following network.

The first network differed from the rest as not all the 'critical friends' had experienced an Action Research Cycle. Network 2 was distinctive in providing a colleague in school with whom the teacher researchers collaborated. However, it transpired that this type of collaboration within the same school did not always lead to effective group discussion as the pair tended to either exclude other members from their deliberations or were indecisive about the subject of their research, or were uncertain about the aspect of research each individual would cover. In the remaining networks, this type of paired collaboration was not pursued.

School Centred Action Networks: Strengths and Weaknesses

In comparing the outcomes of each of the network NGT data; certain common themes emerged as strengths or weaknesses. First, let us consider the strengths.

'*Collaboration*' figured prominently as a strength (although this needed further interpretation, as is later discussed) in the perception of network members in all network evaluations. The data confirmed that participants were enabled to clarify issues, produce ideas, find effective solutions and to gain in self-confidence by opening up their practice to others and sharing expertise.

It was, however, found that at the beginning of each network, an atmosphere conducive to good rapport must be quickly established so that exchange of ideas and constructive criticism may take place. Establishing this rapport proved difficult when support was weak and attendance at meetings irregular. Good collaboration took place more rapidly in single age phase groups (primary/secondary) where there was an established understanding of issues and practicalities.

'*Support*' was identified as a most important factor in achieving successful collaboration. For without support, teacher researchers wasted time talking about irrelevant experiences, lost direction or worried over technique or timing. Experienced supporters enabled researchers to make contributions to discussion, feel valued, understand Action Research techniques, have a sounding board for ideas, clarify their proposals, and reflect on their action steps and evaluations.

In Networks 3, 4 and 5, as the pool of experienced action researchers, grew, so too did support. The data indicated that the participants had uncovered effective ways of helping group collaboration. Supporters were identified and associated with particular researchers, making themselves available not only in meetings but outside and in their own time. Some difficulty was experienced with cross phase groups but this was felt to be more a matter of individual differences rather than a general lack of understanding between primary and secondary colleagues. This finding led to co-ordinators being made more aware of the personal characteristics of their network members in order to match them more carefully with the teacher researchers when organising collaborative groups.

The *'technique'* of Action Research was found to enable teachers to focus on one issue in an organised way. It was seen as a means of changing existing practice resulting in benefits not only to the teacher but also to other colleagues in the school. Whilst it was acknowledged that many teachers evaluate their own practice and devise methods to improve their classroom management or effect changes in whole school policy, it was considered that without the support and structure of a collaborative network, external challenge and validation of interpretations was lacking. Moreover the rigour of regular meetings and an agreed timetable provided by this particular form of networking allowed goals and deadlines to be set and met.

'Professional development' has shown the greatest variation in the perceived strength of electronic action research networking. One interpretation of this variation arises from considering the makeup of the particular network. Networks 1, 2 and 4 had a high proportion of teacher researchers who were either secondary school based or who were using Action Research as part of a modular diploma course and perhaps looking for career moves. In Network 3 and 5 the teacher researchers taking part were not necessarily enrolled on an award bearing course and appeared to focus more closely on issues posed in their school or classroom situation and in the majority of cases, to help a particular child for whom they had specific concerns. Commenting on professional development for teachers, Walker (1985) suggests that

> One view has altruism as its central value and sees teachers' engagement in in-service education as a necessary part of the teaching role. The other view is essentially bureaucratic and some say realistic. It starts with the assumption that teachers attend courses primarily in order to gain qualifications to enhance their career prospects.

The *'outcomes'* or products of the networking system were not only the written reports voluntarily provided by the teacher researchers, but also the impact the action plan was perceived to have had on the school, class or individual child. On either of these interpretations, the outcomes of action research were judged to be a strength.

Network members frequently noted an increased rapport with the subjects of their research, a rapport which was seen to result from improved relationships formed by understanding the problems of children with learning difficulties.

The '*materials*' provided for participants took the form of up-to-date articles selected from a suite of dedicated microcomputer databases. In Networks 1 and 2 these databases were in their early stages of development and there were gaps in the spread of subjects available in the bibliographic database. In Networks 3, 4 and 5 there was a greater demand for materials which was met not only from the database but from resources provided by the linked Higher Education institution. Teacher researchers valued the accessibility of such materials as few schools could afford to purchase research journals and local libraries lacked specialist facilities. In this way, through action research networking, the outcomes of educational research directly informed the decisions of practitioners.

Summary of Strengths

The items listed by network members using the group evaluation structures provided by the nominal group technique, can be categorised under six main themes: collaboration, support, technique, professional development, outcomes and materials. The total number of votes cast for all items identified as strengths in each of the five networks were broadly comparable. The clear consensus of opinion on the strengths of the networking systems centred on the technique of action research with collaboration and support second and third in rank order. An impression of the variation in perceived strengths of each network is represented in figure 7.

Perceived Weaknesses

In the early networks, it was decided not to reveal all the stages of the action cycle in advance to the teacher researchers in case they felt overwhelmed by the demands. The general result was that they tended to be threatened by not knowing what was to happen at the next stage! This led to adaptations introduced in Network 4 when participants were shown reports from the previous network and were given a handbook

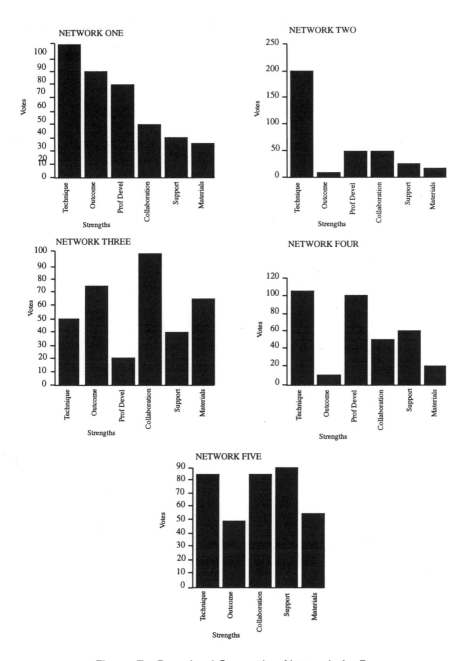

Figure 7   Perceived Strengths, Network 1 – 5

describing each stage of the cycle. It was interesting to note that *'information'* was no longer recorded as a weakness in the evaluations of Networks 4 or 5. It is therefore assumed that this form of network management balances perceived challenge with effective support.

One of the advantages of posing the NGT question in the form of 'Strengths and Weaknesses' is that dominant ideas can be expressed in both positive and negative form leading to a clearer understanding of the issues. For example, 'collaboration' was found to be both a strength and a weakness. In Network 2, the pairing of school colleagues prevented good dialogue and in Network 3 the mixture of secondary and primary phase teachers resulted in weakened co-operation associated with poor attendance at meetings. Collaboration was not however mentioned as a weakness in Networks 4 and 5 perhaps because experienced support was available and greater attention was paid to the *composition* of the groups.

The weaknesses in *'support'* reported in Networks 1 and 2 were largely eliminated in Networks 4 and 5 for by this time a team of supporters were established. This finding may well have been influenced by the continuity of supporters provided through the networking design. It was considered essential that supporters must be experienced in Action Research methods in order for them to have the necessary confidence in their own ability to help colleagues. They needed above all to have good communication skills, knowing when to listen and when to question and how to draw out the more reserved researchers. The supporters found that they needed to acquire methods of group control, allowing each teacher researcher to have time to speak yet knowing how to curtail the more verbose participant.

The weaknesses in *'technique'* recorded in Networks 4 and 5 could arguably be said to have arisen from the success of the Network. Teacher researchers felt they wanted to go deeper into their research subject than the timescale allowed. They also uncovered intriguing side issues which they wanted to investigate further. In Network 5, they would have liked more detailed feedback on their research reports, which again was not practicable in the time allocated.

It will be seen that the use of the group evaluation technique in order to modify each successive network proved effective in reducing perceived weaknesses. However, one issue namely *'time'* was the one predominating weakness which was not eradicated and for which there is no easy solution. The National Curriculum introduced in the U.K. in 1988 has made heavy additional demands on teachers' time. Network members, apart from the co-ordinator who was allocated release time by the LEA, attended voluntarily at meetings which were conducted outside school hours. Data was evaluated, reading done, action steps planned and reports written, entirely in teacher researchers own time. It was, however, interesting to note that they placed such value on this kind of activity that in spite of all the extra work they were being asked to do, they were willing to give time to something that they perceived to be practical, useful for the school and professionally fulfilling.

The action research reports produced by teacher researchers at the end of each network were not eligible for any formal award prior to Network 4. At this point researchers could submit their report as part of a Special Educational Needs Modular Diploma Course offered at a local University. However, the report was only acceptable if the teacher was already enrolled on the course. Those eligible felt that the acceleration for *professional development* was worth far more than the credits actually given.

An impression of the variation in perceived weaknesses is represented in figure 8.

Co-ordinating Action Networks

Finally, it is interesting to compare the experience of the network co-ordinators with the 'dilemmas and temptations of the reflective practitioner' reported from Elliott's (1991) extensive experience of action research and educatiodal change.

He draws six issues to our attention. Evidence of the first of these namely; 'encouraging pupils to critique one's professional practice' was confirmed amongst the network co-ordinators who found a marked reluctance to engage in this form of evaluation except under conditions of strict anonymity. Not only was it rare amongst the network members to seek such data, one co-ordinator remarked that, 'Even as a committed teacher researcher, I personally feel that this could undermine a teacher's standing in the eyes of her students'. Against this, another co-ordinator offered the interpretation that special needs action research is predisposed to specific learning programmes, consequently if a critique were requested of pupils it would most likely focus on the method of teaching used rather than the teacher's performance. However, talk of teacher performance is ambiguous. In one sense, action research could not proceed without some form of evaluation of practice. The central issues are whether such data is direct or indirect, public or private, general (e.g. personality, taste, appearance or social behaviour) or specific (e.g. targeted to individual lessons or identified learning outcomes).

Similar reservations could be made about the second reported dilemma: 'gathering data' (from parents with or without permission from the headteacher). For Elliott's analysis of hierarchical power relations in schools appears to prejudge whether such research could be collaborative. The stereotype offered appears to consign the teacher researcher to the unending task of heroic innovator, wedded first and foremost to the canons of science. Championing the teacher researcher's right to enquire over all other rights would, however, seem to pose certain problems, not least the rejection in advance of the possibility of positive forms of co-operation.

The experience of the five co-ordinators reported here is conditioned by the fact that the networks were conducted by means of an ethical code which required the headteachers' permission to seek data. The logic of collaborative modes of discourse requires this even if statutory and contractual considerations are not deemed to be sufficient criteria. In fact, there were no reports of headteachers unreasonably refusing particular types of data gathering. Network members typically collected data from colleagues, parents, or pupils apparently in spite of, or without experiencing the pathologies portrayed as endemic in relations between teachers and headteachers. In each case, co-operation was forthcoming ranging from active endorsement or involvement to passive acceptance. In several instances, the co-ordinators noted headteachers proceeding to adopt the outcomes of data gathering in formulating or amending school policy. In other cases, however, there was a degree of indifference that was found demotivating to some colleagues. But perhaps these variations could be explained in terms of types of school and their respective cultures, i.e. between primary and secondary schools.

On the reported dilemma of 'sharing data with professional peers both inside and outside the school', network co-ordinators considered that in general the spirit of enquiry engendered by the networks promoted an engagement with critical values rather than deference to authority. However, it did appear that in some cases it was easier to relate to peers outside the school than colleagues; as one co-ordinator commented 'within a school there are divisions of departmental interests, role definitions, and resistance to change that can cause conflict when discussing research data'. In general, the commitment to networking as a means of supporting collaborative action research helped to modify the conflict Elliott ascribes to the 'territorial structure of authority'.

His fourth dilemma draws attention to the temptations of preferring

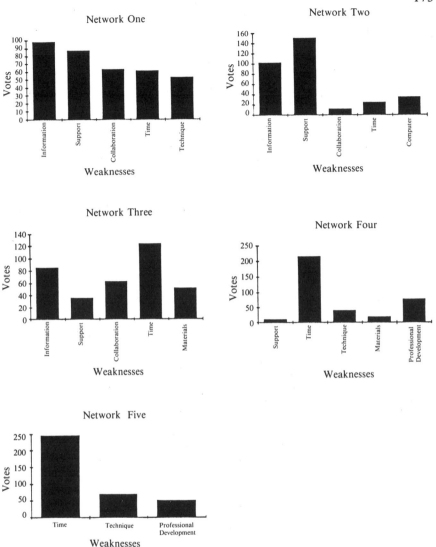

Figure 8   Perceived Weaknesses, Networks 1-5

quantitative data gathering to qualitative approaches 'because the latter involve 'personalised' situations in which colleagues and pupils find it difficult to divorce an individual's position and role as teacher from his/her other positions and roles within the school'.

The co-ordinators' impressions of this dilemma were mixed. Network members were encouraged to triangulate data from at least three sources/types. Where quantitative methods were adopted the ostensible reasons given were that 'they are a familiar tool, demand less time, and are on the whole easier to analyse because the parameters of response can be limited'. The outcomes of such studies, particularly questionnaires, may be no less controversial however. In other cases, qualitative data was gathered and within the confines of small scale research involving one action research cycle, with explicit advocacy of an ethical code, with novitiate action researchers and with the majority of members focusing on individual pupils, the confrontational possibilities were restricted. But so too, it could be argued, was the depth of penetration of the issues explored. And this raises the question as to whether a commitment to action research is primarily for teacher development or school development, or towards the development of an educational knowledge base. These various levels make varying demands. In the case of the action networks, the main concern was to support volunteers who brought a variety of professional experiences to bear, who occupied a wide range of roles within their schools and whose mandates from their schools in joining the networks were widely divergent.

The main problem encountered was not so much which type of data to collect but collecting sufficient data of any kind to usefully interpret in the time made available. As a consequence, not all parts of the action research cycle could be carried out in many cases – as the reports in Part One will testify. But this situation was compensated for in part by the insights of network members collectively sharing and giving encouragement for activities that presently may have had to be postponed.

On the fifth problem of teacher researchers' reluctance 'to produce case studies of their reflective practice except when linked with an award bearing course' this volume demonstrates that such reluctance can be overcome. This is not to say that the issues raised about a prevailing ethos of 'privacy, territoriality and authority' do not present a serious barrier to critical openness or to maintaining the dominance of styles of enquiry other than action research. In the opinion of the co-ordinators, the main stumbling block was the time demand made not simply from writing reports but from the processes of action research overall. Against this, it was acknowledged that the commitment to writing up a report was an important ingredient in getting clear about the nature of the problem/issue being tackled, i.e. it was a necessary condition of sound reflective practice.

Such reluctance as was encountered by co-ordinators arose in part from a professed lack of confidence in writing this type of report for which some had no previous experience or knowledge of audience, or from having to postpone writing to a point in time where recollecting events was less immediate.

However, a desire for recognition of this effort was expressed amongst many network members as Elliott predicts. Such recognition as was formalised through a linked award bearing course where this applied was considered minimal and where this route did not apply, the general feeling was one of isolation. Here, however, the existence of a network greatly helped to promote solidarity and a sense of being valued.

In other cases, the particular circumstances of special needs pupils, the amount of data to analyse within the given timescale, the slow rate of change observed as a result of action steps, and the perceived problem of reporting negative results, were all evident in reactions to producing reports.

The experience of the networks generally confirmed the view that interpretations of research based teaching could be usefully shared with colleagues and that the activity itself, although largely centred on individual interests, was greatly enhanced through discussions with colleagues. In these ways, the fact of membership of a network may have been instrumental in overcoming such minor reservations as were encountered.

Finally, Elliott comments: 'The problem of time for insider research tends to be viewed as a teaching v research dilemma which gets resolved in favour of the former.'

In the case of the networks, this issue dominated throughout, especially from Network 3 onwards. It is tempting to speculate that this reflects the extra demands on teachers arising from the National Curriculum. The co-ordinators' attempts to ameliorate this situation culminated in release time being given by the LEA for classroom based support for network activities. Whilst this effort was much appreciated by teachers, it appeared to increase the appetite for more of the same.

Thus, although the co-ordinators' experience confirmed Elliott's view that: 'Membership of ... a network can provide the kind of mutual resources which strengthen the capacity of aspiring teacher researchers to resist the time pressures operating on them from inside their schools', the problem persisted and greatly affected the researchers' estimate of their effectiveness and the ultimate value of their work. The fact that much of this research was actually carried out in the teachers 'own time' suggests that at least in these instances, the prevailing ethos of teaching however described, was not a determining influence.

Another interpretation was expressed by one co-ordinator in other terms: 'Teachers of children with special needs always spend considerable time planning alternative programme of work, liaising with outside agencies to find alternative methods of teaching and learning. If the teacher isn't prepared to spend this additional time on preparation, implementation and evaluation, the pupils are simply "Trouble"!'

Conclusion

Action Research generated such enthusiasm among participants in the networks that they maintained contact with subsequent networks as supporters or consultants or embarked on further research. The perceived friendliness of the networks and the continuity of membership were especially appreciated by teachers of children with special educational needs. Such teachers often felt isolated and overburdened with the problems of enabling access to the curriculum to children with physical handicap, learning difficulties or behavioural problems. Answers to such problems were found by sharing expertise or simply by allowing themselves time to concentrate on a particular issue. This form of critical discourse raises intriguing questions about the possibilities for building an intercultural pedagogy in the new Europe. For as the ideology of nationalism comes to be recognised as a necessary rather than sufficient condition for preparing pupils for an increasingly interdependent world, structures of communication of this type (already operating in the global commercial information networks) may be seen to have a crucial role to play in moves towards a transnational dimension to educational development.

These are the 'crossroads' that colleagues in other European countries also refer to: what Vonk (1991) describes as the 'bureaucratic-managerial' v 'professional' approach and Elliott sees as the traditional craft culture of teaching constraining the emergence of professional values including those of reflective practice and their systematic development through action research.

It remains to be seen how the role of the teacher will unfold over the coming decade. This book meanwhile has indicated ways in which teachers can contribute to knowledge of their own practice whether operating within a professional or 'bureaucratic-managerial' culture. Whilst the latter influences prevail, predominantly in England, there is much that can be negotiated to encompass the values of action research, most notably through seeing connections with procedures for school development planning, and the newly introduced framework for inspection.

But as the sources of external support for teachers dwindle whether through dismemberment of LEA's or Teacher Training departments or reductions in funds for INSET, the scale of the challenge will increase. New ways of interpreting these circumstances will have to be found. In so far as school autonomy enables federalist principles to take root (Handy, 1992) i.e. of placing power at the lowest point of a hierarchy, of spreading power around in order to encourage interdependence, of exploiting the positive features of a common law and language as the National Curriculum now provides, of keeping management, monitoring and governance in segregated units, and recognising that federal institutions have multiple loyalties not least to an international if not European community, the prospects for school development through action research are less dim than might be imagined.

The chief hope of the contributors therefore is that it will offer a positive view of school leadership. But above all, it is hoped that it will act as a reminder that schools themselves have the choice of transforming their present arrangements, grouped as they frequently are in 'families' and 'clusters' to form the kinds of networks that are discussed here. It is our contention that, in the jargon of the moment, they will both 'add value' and be 'cost effective', providing an underwriting insurance when things go wrong and validating best practice when things go right. In this way, the goal of building a truly educational community by securing access to a common curriculum for all will most surely be realised.

APPENDIX 1

OBSERVATION SHEET

DATE   ROLL   _____

ACTIVITIES: 'WAITING GAME' – WG   '101 WAYS' – 101
             'RULES'   – R   'CARDS'   – C
             'NAME GAME'   – NG   'THANKS' – T
             'BRAINSTORM' – BR

TIME	PUPIL	GROUP	TEACHER	COMMENT
11.00				

GENERAL COMMENTS

OOS – out of seat   TL – talking loudly SH – shouting
DO – disturbing others   OFT – off task   OT – on task
DT disturbing teacher TIC – teacher initiated contact

N.B. Do not forget to record both positive and negative pupils

APPENDIX 2
Lesson Plans for Circle Time Through Drama

DRAMA SESSIONS

AIMS

a) To give each pupil a chance to learn more about themselves through drama techniques.
b) To show use of various control techniques within the Circle Session.
c) To highlight positive teaching techniques.
d) To give each pupil the chance to use language in specific controlled circumstances.
e) To specifically look at grouping structures within the class and their affect on individual behaviour.

SESSION ONE

ACTIVITIES .... (give a brief outline)

Waiting Game	– this game allows the leader to see how long the group takes to get ready to work.
Rules	– to make it clear to all that there are activity specific rules. Re-establish clearly!
My Friend	– each person to talk, if they wish about their friend(s).
Groups	– a brainstorm about Groups.
101 Ways	– a different grouping involved in a lateral thinking exercise. 101 things to do with a ball of string, a plastic bag and a Swiss Army knife. Situation is a Tropical Island.
Person Who	– a whole group truth game. The first set should contain 'positive' statements.

SESSION TWO

ACTIVITIES .... (give a brief outline)

Waiting Game — this game allows the leader to see how long the group takes to get ready to work.

Rules — to make it clear to all that there are Activity specific rules. Re-establish clearly!

My Favourite — each person to talk, if they wish about their favourite . . .

Groups — a brainstorm about Groups.

101 Ways — a different grouping involved in a lateral thinking exercise. 101 things to do with a box of candles, a bag of balloons, a Swiss Army knife. Situation is a cave.

Person Who — a whole group truth game. The first set should contain 'positive' statements.

On The Spot — a card game that gives control of the game to one person. Various questions which give the chance for the individual to talk about themselves.

ORGANISATIONAL AND GAME STRATEGIES

a) Waiting — wait for quiet, utilise group, peer pressure.
b) Timing — clearly set out the time framework.
c) Inform — clearly inform as to the activities.
d) Stopping — if the noise level is too high, or individuals are interfering with others, stop and wait for stillness, DO NOT cast judgement on individuals.
e) Praise — pick up on all GOOD elements of work, social behaviour, sensible noise levels, etc. Make it a group praise, not an individual praise as we are primarily looking at working in a group!
f) Restart — do not be frightened to stop the session and seat the children on the carpet and restart. YOU are in total control of the management of the class and that fact must be clear to ALL pupils.

APPENDIX 3
Proposed Check List for Lesson Observations

Pupil Ownership of Lesson

Setting	Teacher Directed				Pupil Directed
Setting Task	*	*	*	*	*
Organising	*	*	*	*	*
Task	*	*	*	*	*
Running the task	*	*	*	*	*

Recording of Achievement   Yes/No

Individual . . . .

Pairs . . . .

Informal . . . .

Formal . . . .

Mixed Ability . . . .

Selected Ability . . . .

Mixed Sex . . . .

Selective Sex Groupings . . . .

Effective Use of Resources

	A Great	Deal			Little Use
Teacher as a resource	*	*	*	*	*
Pupils as a resource	*	*	*	*	*

Outside Agent   *   *   *   *   *
(Please specify)

. . . .

. . . .

Does the resource enhance discrimination learning?

                 *   *   *   *   *

Provide
sub-skills   *   *   *   *   *

Opportunity for   *   *   *   *   *
independent
work

Use of text   *   *   *   *   *
books

Duplicated ma-   *   *   *   *   *
terial Provided
by Staff

Pupil collected   *   *   *   *   *
material

Classroom Management

Arrangement of desks   Rows   —   Individual
                                  Rows   —   Pairs
                                  Groups   —   Pairs
                                  Groups   —   Fours

Layout of Classroom

Extensive   Limited
  *   *   *   *   *

Relevant   Old
  *   *   *   *   *

GLOSSARY

Aston Index:	System of diagnostic testing of various sub-skills to reading.
Basic Tests in English:	Associated Examination Board test based on business skills, appropriate for pupils 16 and over.
Breakthrough to Literacy:	Primary School Language Development Programme. Longmans Educational.
Concept Keyboard:	Added facility to aid computer operation for pupils with physical and/or learning difficulties.
C.R.O.W.N.:	Reading development package produced by Hull Learning Support Services.
Derbyshire Language Manual:	An approach to teaching language to children who are severely impaired.
Dyslexia Institute:	Institute based at 133, Gresham Road, Staines, Middlesex, TW18 2AJ, concerned with the diagnostic and reading development skills of pupils who have reading and writing problems.
Folio:	Computer based writing programme.
Fuzzbuzz:	A commercially produced reading scheme.
G.C.S.E.:	General Certificate of Education. Examination taken by pupils at age of 16.
Hull Basic Sounds Vocabulary:	Produced by Hull Learning Support Service (Humberside LEA)
INSET:	Inservice education for teachers.
Keywords Scheme:	Lists of keywords most commonly used in reading, e.g. Ladybird Wordlists.
LEA:	Local Education Authority.
Living Language Programme:	An oral language programme for pupils with learning difficulties.
LMS:	Local Management of Schools. A system by which individual schools can manage their own finances.
Paired Reading:	A system of shared reading to help pupils with reading problems on an individual basis with one other helper, often a parent or relation.

P.I.T.C.H.	A test of phonic knowledge produced by Hull Learning Support Service (Humberside L.E.A.).
PSD:	Personal and Social Development.
PMAT:	Perceptual Motor Abilities Test in Lazlo et al (1988).
Reading Age:	A way of measuring level of reading ability often compared with the chronological (actual) age of reader.
Richardson, M.:	Style of handwriting often taught in primary schools.
SEN:	Special Educational Needs.
S.M.P.:	Scottish Maths Project Programme.
S.N.A.P.:	Special Needs Action Programme.
Starspell:	Computer Board Programme to aid spelling development produced by Hummec. (Humberside Microelectronics Centre).
Spar Spelling Test:	Test of Spelling Skills produced by Hodder and Stoughton Educational, London.
S.P.M.G.:	Scottish Primary Maths Group.
S.A.T.:	Standard Assessment Tests. Government based Assessment tests taken by pupils at ages 7, 11, 14 and 16.
TOMI:	Test of Motor Impairment (1984) devised by Stott, D.H., Moyes, F.A., Henderson, S.E. (1984) Guelph, Ontario: Brook Educational.
WISC:	Weschler Intelligence Scale for Children.

BIBLIOGRAPHY

Alvin, J. (1976) *Music for the Handicapped Child* (2nd ed). Oxford: Oxford University Press.

Ainslie, J. (1982) 'Teaching Reading Comprehension: A Different Perspective' *Remedial Education*, Vol.17 pp.171–173. London: Longmans.

Alston, J. and Taylor J. (1987) *Handwriting Theory, Research and Practice*, London: Croom Helm.

Aronowitz, S. and Giroux, H.A. (1986) *Education Under Seige: The Conservative, Liberal and Radical Debate over Schooling*, London: Routledge and Kegan Paul.

Bell, G.H. and Dennis, S. (1991) '*Special Needs Development, Networking and Managing for Change; European Journal of Special Needs Education*, Vol. 6 No 2 pp 133–40.

Bell G.H. (1985) *Can Schools Develop Knowledge of Their Practice?' School Organisation* 5, 2 pp 175–184.

Bell, G.H. and Pennington, R.C. (1987) '*Action Learning and School Focused Study', Collected Original Resources in Education*, Vol.12, No. 1

Bell, G.H. (1988) in J.Nias and S.Groundwater Smith (Eds), *The Enquiring Teacher*. Lewes: The Falmer Press.

Beresford, C.R. and Bridges, D. (1980) '*School Centred World' Journal of Applied Educational Studies* 9, 1, pp.5–12.

Bereiter, C and Engleman, S. (1966) *Teaching Disadvantaged Children in the Pre-School*, London: Prentice Hall.

Bernstein, B. (1971) *Class Codes and Control* (Vol.1). London: Routledge and Kegan Paul.

Borba, M. and Borba, C. (1982) *Self Esteem: A Classroom Affair* (Vol 2). London: Harper Collins.

Bowlby, J. (1953) *Childcare and the Growth of Love*. London: Penguin.

Branwhite, R. (ed) (1990) *Classroom Organisation for Special Needs*. Beverley, Humberside, L.E.A.

Bruner, J.S. (1966) *Toward a Theory of Instruction*. New York: Norton.

Camsey, J. (1985) 'Taking Leave' in *Junior Education* (July Edition) Leamington Spa: Scholastic Publications.

Chazan, M. (1991) *Helping Five to Eight Year Olds with Special Education Needs*. London: Blackwell.

Cotterell, G. (1985): *Teaching the Non Reading Dyslexic Child*. London: Learning Development Aids.

Cripps, C. and Peters, M. (1991) *Catchwords*. London: Harcourt Brace.

Cripps, C. (1983): 'A Report of an Experiment to see whether Young Children can be taught to Work from Memory'. *Remedial Education*. Vol.18 (i) p.19-24. London: Longmans.

Delbecq, A.L. Van de Ven, A.H., Gustafson, D.H. (1975): *Group Techniques for Program Planning: a Guide to Nominal and Delphi Processes*. Glen View, Illinois: Scott Foresman.

Dennis, S (1988) in D.Smith, (Ed) *New Technologies and Professional Communications in Education*. National Council for Educational Technology.

Department of Education and Science. (1985) *The Curriculum from 5-16*, London: HMSO

Diniz F.A. (1991) 'Special Education: an Overview of Recent Changes', *European Journal of Teacher Education*, Vol.14 No.2 pp. 107-115.

Durkin, D. (1966) *Children Who Read Early: Two Longitudinal Studies*. New York: Teachers College Press.

Elliott J. (1978) 'What is Action Research in Schools?' *Journal of Curriculum Studies 10*, pp.355-7.

Elliott J. (1991) *Action Research for Educational Change*. Milton Keynes: Open University.

Elton Report (1989) *Discipline in Schools*. London: HMSO.

Fisher, C. (undated) *Positive Approaches to Behavioural Problems*. Issued by Doncaster Local Education Authority.

Fraser, E.D. (1959) *Home Environment and the School*. Edinburgh: Hodder.

Francis, H. (1975) *Language in Childhood: Form and Function in Language Learning*. London: Elek.

Freire, P. (1977) *Education for Critical Consciousness*. New York: Seabury Press.

Gillham, (1979) *First Words Language Programme: A Basic Language Programme for Mentally Handicapped Children*. London: Allen and Unwin.

Gorwood, B.T. (1985) *School Transfer and Curriculum Continuity*. London: Croom Helm.

Guba, E. and Lincoln, Y.S. (1989) *Fourth Generation Evaluation*. London: Sage.

Hall, M. (1986) Unpublished, dissertation for Diploma in Professional Studies in Education. Sheffield Polytechnic.

Handy, C. (1992) 'Balancing Corporate Power: New Federalist Paper,' *Harvard Business Review* 1992 Nov/Dec issue Vol. 70 no.6 pp. 59–72.

Hargie, O. (Ed) (1989) *A Handbook of Communication Skills*. London: Routledge.

Hargie, O. Saunders, C. and Dickson, D. (1981) *Social Skills in Interpersonal Communication*. London: Croom Helm.

Hewison, J. and Tizard, J. (1980) 'Parental Involvement and Reading Attainment'. *British Journal of Educational Psychology*, Vol.50 para.3 pp.209–215.

Hopson, B. and Scally, M. (1980) *Lifeskills Teaching*. London: McGraw Hill.

Humberside County Council, (1985) *Establishing a Guidance Programme to Promote Personal and Social Development*. Beverley, Humberside. County Council Education Department.

Illich I. (1973) *Deschooling Society*. Harmondsworth: Penquin.

Inhelder, B. and Piaget, J. (1958) *The Growth of Logical Thinking from Childhood to Adolescence*. New York: Basic Books.

I.L.E.A. (1985) *Improving Primary Schools*. Inner London Education Authority.

Jarman, C. (1979) *Development of Handwriting Skills: A Book of Resources for Teachers*, (1) Oxford: Blackwell.

Johnson, C. and Jenkinson, H. (1915) *English Court Hand A.D. 1066–1500*. Oxford: Blackwell.

Jones, S. (1990) 'The Genealogy of the Urban School Teacher' in Ball, S. (Ed) (1990) *Foucault and Education, Disciplines and Knowledge*. London: Routledge pp.57–77.

Kazamais, A.M. (1990) *The Curse of Sisyphus in Greek Educational Reform: A Social-Political and Cultural Interpretation*. University of Minnesota. Greek Yearbook pp. 1–20.

Laszlo, J. Barstow, R. and Bartrip, J.B (1988) *A New Approach in Support for Learning*, Vol. 3 (i) p.35–40. London: Longmans.

Louis, K.S. and Rosenblum, S. (1981) *Designing and Managing Interorganisational Networks: Linking R and D with Schools*. National Institute of Education, Washington, D.C. Dissemination and Improvement of Practice Programme.

Lytton, H. (1968) *School Counselling and Counsellor Education in the United States*. Slough: N.F.E.R.

Male, J. and Thompson, C. (1985) *The Educational Implications of Disability: A Guide for Teachers.* London Royal Association for Disability and Rehabilitation.

Manders, J. (1987) Unpublished Teacher Researcher Study conducted on one Primary School.

Maude, B. (1974) *Practical Communication for Managers.* London: Longmans.

McCarthy, T. (1978) *The Critical Theory of Jurgen Habermas.* London: Hutchinson.

McCormick, R. and James, M. (1988) *Curriculum Evaluation in Schools.* 2nd Ed. London: Croom Helm.

McNally, J. and Murray, W. (1968) *Keywords to Literacy.* London: Schoolmaster Publishing Company.

Measor, L. and Woods, P. (1984) *Changing Schools: Pupil Perspectives on Transfer to a Comprehensive.* Milton Keynes: Open Univ. Press.

Mitter, W. (Ed) (1991) 'Teacher Education in Europe: Problems, Challenges, Perspectives.' *British Journal of Educational Studies.* Vol. XXXIX No.2 May pp.138–152.

Mortimore, P. et al (1988) *School Matters: The Junior Years.* Wells: Open Books.

Mutusiak, C. (1988) *Shared Records for Pre-Fives in Child Education* (December) pp.13–15.

National Association for Remedial Education (1988) *Parents as Partners.* Guide-Lines No 7. Stafford N.A.R.E.

Nash, R. (1973) *Classrooms Observed.* London: Routledge and Kegan Paul.

Newsom, J. and Newsom, E. (1963) *Infant Care in an Urban Community.* London: Allen and Unwin.

OECD (1989) *Schools and Quality: An International Report.* Paris: OECD

O'Leary, K.D. and O'Leary, S.G. (1977) *Classroom Management: The Successful Use of Behaviour Modification* New York: Pergamon Press.

Peters, M. (1985) *Spelling Caught or Taught? A New Look* (Rev.Ed). London: Routledge and Kegan Paul.

Piaget, J. (1952): *The Child's Conception of Number.* London: Routledge and Kegan Paul.

Piers E.V. and Harris D. (1969) *Children's Self Concept Scale*: Counsellor Recordings.

Reynolds, M. (1976) 'The Delinquent School' in M. Hammersley and P. Woods, (eds) *The Process of Schooling: A Sociological Reader.* London: Routledge and Kegan Paul.

Rogers, E.M. and Shoemaker, F.F. (1971) *Communication of Innovations, A Cross Cultural Approach*. New York: Collier-MacMillan.

Rutter, M., Maughan B, Mortimore, P. Ouston, J.M (1979) *Fifteen thousand hours: Secondary Schools and Their Effects on Children*. London: Open Books.

Sassoon, R. (1982) *The Practical Guide to Calligraphy*. London: Thames and Hudson.

Shipman,. M.D., Bolam, D., Jenkins, D.R., (1974) *Inside a Curriculum Project*. London: Methuen.

Smith, J. (1985): *Transferring to Secondary School*. Home and School Publications.

Stakes, J. R. (1988) 'An Investigation into the Effects of the Warnock Report and the Associated Documentation on the Organisation and Provision for Pupils with Special Educational Needs in the Mainstream Secondary School'. Unpublished PhD Thesis, University of Hull.

Stenhouse, L. (1975) *An Introduction to Curriculum Research and Development*. London: Heinemann

Stenhouse, L. (1979) 'Using Research Means doing Research' in H.Dahl, A.Lysne and P.Rand (Eds). *A Spotlight on Education Problems, Festchrift for Johannes Sandven*, Oslo University Press.

Tizzard, B., Mortimore, J., and Burchell, B. (1980) *Involving Parents in Nursery and Infant Schools: A Source Book for Teachers*. London: Grant McIntyre.

Topping, K.J., McKnight, G. (1984) 'Paired Reading and Parent Power' *Special Education*, Vol.II, No.3 Sept. pp. 12–15.

Topping, K.J. (1987) *The Peer Tutoring Handbook*. London: Croom Helm.

Topping, K.J. (1987) 'Peer Tutors Paired Reading Outcomes: Data from Ten Projects'. *Educational Psychology*, Vol.7 (ii).

Vernon, M.D. (1971) *Reading and its Difficulties: A Psychological Study*. London: Cambridge University Press.

Vonk, H. (1991) 'Some Trends in the Development of Curricula for the Professional Preparation of Primary and Secondary School Teachers: A Comparative Study.' *British Journal of Educational Studies*. Vol. XXXIX No. 2 May pp 117/137.

Vulliamy, G. and Webb R. (Eds) (1992) *Teacher Research and Special Educational Needs*. London: David Fulton Publishers.

Vygotsky, L.S. (1962) *Thought and Language*. Cambridge (Mass). M.I.T. Press.

Walker, R. (1985) *Doing Research: A Handbook for Teachers*. London: Methuen.

Warnock, M. (Chairman) (1978) *Special Educational Needs*: Report of the Committee of Enquiry into the Education of Handicapped Children and Young People. London: H.M.S.O

Westwood, P.S. (1975) *The Remedial Teacher's Handbook*. Edinburgh: Oliver & Boyd.

Williams, A. (1970) *Basic Subjects for the Slow Learner*. London: Methuen.

Williamson, C. and Williamson, J. (1986): 'A Recipe for Success' in *Support for Learning 1* (iii) (August) pp.13–18.

Youngman, M.B. (ed) (1986) *Mid Schooling Transfer: Problems and Proposals*. Windsor: NFER-Nelson.

INDEX

Caerleon
Library